Economic Issues and Development

CONTEMPORARY NATIVE AMERICAN ISSUES

Economic Issues and Development

Deborah Welch
Director of the Public History Program/
Associate Professor of History, Longwood University

Foreword by
Walter Echo-Hawk
Senior Staff Attorney, Native American Rights Fund

Introduction by
Paul Rosier
Assistant Professor of History, Villanova University

CHELSEA HOUSE
PUBLISHERS
A Haights Cross Communications Company ®
Philadelphia

CHELSEA HOUSE PUBLISHERS

VP, NEW PRODUCT DEVELOPMENT Sally Cheney
DIRECTOR OF PRODUCTION Kim Shinners
CREATIVE MANAGER Takeshi Takahashi
MANUFACTURING MANAGER Diann Grasse

Staff for ECONOMIC ISSUES AND DEVELOPMENT

EXECUTIVE EDITOR Lee Marcott
EDITOR Christian Green
PRODUCTION EDITOR Bonnie Cohen
PHOTO EDITOR Sarah Bloom
SERIES AND COVER DESIGNER Takeshi Takahashi
LAYOUT EJB Publishing Services

A Haights Cross Communications ✦ Company ®

www.chelseahouse.com

First Printing

9 8 7 6 5 4 3 2 1

Library of Congress Cataloging-in-Publication Data
Welch, Deborah, 1952–
   Economic issues and development / Deborah Welch.
      p. cm. — (Contemporary Native American issues)
   Includes bibliographical references and index.
   ISBN 0-7910-7973-2 (hard cover)
  1. Indians of North America—Economic conditions—Juvenile
literature. I. Title. II. Series.
  E98.E2W45 2005
  330.9'0089'9707—dc22

                     2005007545

Contents

Foreword

◈ · ◈ · ◈

Walter Echo-Hawk

Native Americans share common aspirations, and a history and fate with indigenous people around the world. International law defines indigenous peoples as non-European populations who resided in lands colonized by Europeans before the colonists arrived. The United Nations estimates that approximately 300 million persons worldwide are variously known as tribal, Native, aboriginal, or indigenous. From 1492 to 1945, European nations competed to conquer, colonize, and Christianize the rest of the world. Indigenous peoples faced a difficult, life-altering experience, because colonization invariably meant the invasion of their homelands, appropriation of their lands, destruction of their habitats and ways of life, and sometimes genocide.

Though colonialism was repudiated and most colonies achieved independence, the circumstances of indigenous peoples has not improved in countries where newly independent nations adopted the preexisting colonial system for dealing with indigenous peoples. In such nations, colonial patterns still exist. The paramount challenge to human rights in these nations, including our own, is to find just ways to protect the human, political, cultural, and property rights of their indigenous people.

Contemporary issues, including those of culture, can be understood against the backdrop of colonialism and the closely related need to strengthen laws to protect indigenous rights. For example, colonists invariably retained close cultural ties to their distant homelands and rarely adopted their indigenous neighbors' values, cultures, or ways of looking at Mother Earth. Instead, they imposed their cultures, languages, and religions upon tribal people through the use of missionaries, schools, soldiers, and governments.

In the mid-1800s, U.S. government policymakers used the "Vanishing Red Man" theory, which was advanced by anthropologists at the time, as justification for the forcible removal of Native American tribes and for taking their lands. The policy did not work; America's indigenous peoples did not "vanish" as predicted. Native American tribes are still here despite suffering great difficulties since the arrival of Europeans, including an enormous loss of life and land brought on by disease, warfare, and genocide. Nonetheless, diverse groups survived, thrived, and continue to be an important part of American society.

Today, Native Americans depend on domestic law to protect their remaining cultural integrity but often that law is weak and ill-suited for the task, and sometimes does not exist at all. For example, U.S. federal law fails to protect indigenous holy places, even though other nations throughout the world take on the responsibility of protecting sacred sites within their borders. Congress is aware of this loophole in religious liberty but does not remedy it. Other laws promote assimilation, like the "English only" laws that infringe upon the right of Native Americans to retain their indigenous languages.

Another example concerns indigenous property rights. The *very* purpose of colonialism was to provide riches, property, and resources for European coffers. To that end, a massive one-way transfer of property from indigenous to nonindigenous hands occurred in most colonies. This included land, natural resources, and personal property (called *artifacts* by anthropologists). Even dead bodies (called *specimens* or *archaeological resources* by anthropologists) were dug up and carried away. The appropriation has been extended to intellectual property: aboriginal plant and animal knowledge patented by corporations; tribal names, art, and symbols converted into trademarks; and religious beliefs and practices *borrowed* by members of the New Age movement. Even tribal identities have been taken by "wannabes" masquerading as Native Americans for personal, professional, or commercial gain. In beleaguered Native eyes, little else is left to take. Native legal efforts attempt to stem and reverse this one-way transfer of property and protect what little remains.

Through it all, Native American tribes have played an important role in the American political system. The U.S. Constitution describes the political relationships among the federal government, states, Native American tribes, and foreign nations. Hundreds of tribal governments comprise our political system as "domestic dependent nations." They exercise power over Native American reservations, provide for their tribal citizens, engage in economic development, and sometimes come into conflict with states over intergovernmental disputes. Many tribes own and manage vast tracts of tribal land, extensive water rights, and other natural resources. The United States holds legal title to this property in trust. As trustee, the United States exercises significant power over the lives of Native Americans and their communities; and it is responsible for their well-being. These "nations within nations" are not found on international maps and are invisible to many in our own country.

Prior to 1900, about five hundred treaties between Native American tribes and the United States were duly ratified by the Senate and signed into law by the president. Treaties contain hard-fought agreements that were earned on American battlefields and made between Native American tribes and the United States. They opened vast expanses of Native American land to white settlement, protected remaining Native property, and created the political relationships with the U.S. government that remain to this day. As President George H.W. Bush said during his inaugural address in 1989, "great nations like great men must keep their word." Though many treaties were broken, many promises are honored by the United States today and upheld by federal courts.

The history, heritage, and aspirations of Native Americans create many challenges today. Concern for tribal sovereignty, self-determination, and cultural survival are familiar among Native Americans. Their struggles to protect treaty rights (such as hunting, fishing, and gathering rights), achieve freedom of religion, and protect Mother Earth (including land, resources, and habitat) are commonplace challenges, and sometimes include the task of repatriating dead relatives from museums. Each year, Congress passes laws affecting vital Native interests and the Supreme Court decides crucial cases. The hardships that Native Americans have endured to keep their identity are little known to many Americans. From the times of Red Cloud, Seattle, and Chief Joseph, Native leaders have fought to achieve these freedoms for their people. These ideals even today motivate many Native American soldiers to fight for our country in distant lands, like Iraq and Afghanistan, with the hope that the principles fought for abroad will be granted to their relatives at home.

Today, vibrant Native American communities make significant contributions to our rich national heritage. Evidence of this can be found in the recently opened National Museum of the American Indian, in Washington, D.C. It is also found throughout the pages of *Native Peoples* magazine and other Native media. It fills the best galleries, museums, and auction houses. It can be seen in the art, dance, music, philosophy, religion, literature, and film made by Native Americans, which rank among the world's finest. Visitors crowd tribal casinos and other enterprises that dot Native American reservations in growing numbers. Tribal governments, courts, and agencies are more sophisticated than ever before. Native American-controlled schools and colleges are restoring the importance of culture, traditions, and elders in education, and instill Native pride in students. The determination to retain indigenous cultures can be seen through the resurgence of tribal language, culture, and religious ceremonial life.

Yet many old problems persist. Too many Native Americans are impoverished and in poor health; living at the very bottom of almost all socioeconomic indicators and often in violence-ridden communities where disease, such as AIDS, knows no racial or cultural boundaries. Some socioeconomic problems stem from the aftermath of colonization of Native lands, peoples, and resources, or from efforts to stamp out Native culture and religion. Others stem from prejudice and hostility against Native people that has long characterized race relations in the United States.

As our nation matures, we must reject, once and for all, harmful policies and notions of assimilation and ethnocentrism, and embrace cultural relativism in our relations with the Native peoples who comprise our diverse society. History teaches where racial stereotypes, myths, and fictions prevail, human rights violations soon follow. But social change comes slowly and ethnocentrism remains deeply rooted in mass media and other corners of society. To little avail, Native people have told Hollywood to stop stereotyping Native Americans, protested against harmful racial stereotypes used by groups like the "Redskin" football team, and requested appropriate coverage of Native issues by the mainstream media. Native life is far different than how it has been depicted in the movies and by school and professional mascots.

Regrettably, schools do not teach us about Native Americans; textbooks largely ignore the subject. Sidebar information is provided only when Pilgrims or other American heroes are discussed, but Native Americans mostly "disappear" after dining with Pilgrims, leaving students to wonder about their fate. As a result, the people who met Columbus, Coronado, Custer, and Lewis and Clark are still here, but remain a mystery to legislators, policymakers, and judges who decide vital Native interests. Those interests are too often overlooked, marginalized, or subordinated by the rest of society. The widespread lack of education and information is the most serious problem confronting America's Native people today.

CONTEMPORARY NATIVE AMERICAN ISSUES will help remedy the information gap and enable youth to better understand the issues mentioned above. We are fortunate to have comprehensive data compiled in this series for students. Armed with facts, this generation can address Native American challenges justly.

Walter R. Echo-Hawk
Boulder, Colorado
March 2005

Introduction

Paul Rosier

During the mid-1970s, I attended Swarthmore High School in suburban Philadelphia, Pennsylvania. There, I learned little about Native Americans other than that they had lived in teepees, hunted buffalo, and faced great hardships in adapting to modern life at the end of the nineteenth century. But I learned nothing about Native Americans' experiences in the twentieth century. And as a member of the Tomahawks, the high school football team, I was constantly reminded that Native Americans had been violent and had used primitive weapons like tomahawks. Movies and television shows reinforced these notions in my young and impressionable mind.

It is my experience from teaching Native American history at the university level that students in middle and high schools across the country, have not, with some exceptions, learned much more about Native Americans in the twentieth century than I did thirty years ago. Several years ago, one of my students asked me if Native Americans still live in tepees. He and many others like him continue to be presented with a limited and biased interpretation of Native Americans, largely from popular culture, especially sports, where professional teams, such as the Washington Redskins, and mascots, such as the University of Illinois' Chief Illiniwek, continue to portray Native Americans as historical objects, not as citizens of this nation and as members of distinct tribal communities.

In 1990, President George H.W. Bush approved a joint resolution of Congress that designated November National Indian Heritage Month, and over the following years similar proclamations were made by presidents William J. Clinton and George W. Bush. On November 1, 1997, President Clinton stated: "As we enter the next millennium we have an exciting opportunity to open a new era of understanding, cooperation, and respect among all of America's people. We must work together to tear down the walls of separation and mistrust and build a strong foundation for the future." In November 2001, President Bush echoed Clinton by saying, "I call on all Americans to learn more about the history and heritage of the Native peoples of this great land. Such actions reaffirm our appreciation and respect for their traditions and way of life and can help to preserve an important part of our culture for generations yet to come."

We still have work to do to further "understanding, cooperation, and respect among all of America's people" and to "learn more about the history and heritage of the Native peoples of this great land." The information presented in CONTEMPORARY NATIVE AMERICAN ISSUES is designed to address the challenges set forth by presidents Clinton and Bush, and debunk the inaccurate perceptions of Native Americans that stretches back to our nation's founding and continues today. For example, schoolchildren's first intellectual exposure to Native Americans may well be through the Declaration of Independence, which describes Native Americans as "merciless Indian savages, whose known rule of warfare is an undistinguished destruction of all ages, sexes, and conditions."

The series' authors are scholars who have studied and written about the issues that affect today's Native Americans. Each scholar committed to write for this series because they share my belief that educating our youth about Native Americans should begin earlier in our schools and that the subject matter should be presented accurately.

Outside the classroom, young students' first visual exposure to Native Americans likely comes from sporting contests or in popular culture. First impressions matter. C. Richard King, Associate Professor of Comparative Ethnic Studies at Washington State University, discusses this important issue in his volume, *Media Images and Representations*. King looks at how these early impressions of Native Americans persist in film and television, journalism, sports mascots, indigenous media, and the internet. But he also looks at how Native Americans themselves have protested these images and tried to create new ones that more accurately reflect their history, heritage, and contemporary attitudes.

In *Education and Language Restoration*, Jon Allan Reyhner examines the history of how Native Americans have been educated in boarding schools or mission schools to become assimilated into mainstream American society. Reyhner, Professor of Education at Northern Arizona University, considers how Native Americans have recently created educational systems to give students the opportunity to learn about their culture and to revitalize dormant languages. Like non-Native American students, Native students should invest time and energy in learning about Native American culture and history.

This educational process is important to help Native Americans deal with a myriad of social problems that affects many communities in our country. In their volume *Social Life and Issues*, Roe Walker Bubar and Irene S. Vernon, professors at the Center for Applied Studies in American Ethnicity at Colorado State University, review the various social issues that Native Americans face, including health problems like AIDS and alcoholism. They also consider how Native American communities try to resolve these social and health crises by using traditional healing ceremonies and religious practices that are hundreds of years old.

One very important issue that has helped Native American communities heal is repatriation. Joe Edward Watkins, Associate Professor of Anthropology at the University of New Mexico, examines this significant matter in his volume, *Sacred Sites and Repatriation*. Repatriation involves the process of the government returning to individual tribes the remains of ancestors stolen from graves in the nineteenth century, as well as pots and ceremonial objects also taken from graves or stolen from reservations. Native Americans have fought for the return of objects and remains but also to protect sacred sites from being developed. Such places have religious or spiritual meaning and their protection is important to ensure continued practice of traditional ceremonies that allow Native Americans to address the social and health problems that Vernon and Bubar describe.

In *Political Issues*, Deborah Welch, the Director of the Public History Program and Associate Professor of History at Longwood University, writes about how Native Americans reclaimed political power and used it to strengthen their communities through legislation that promoted both repatriation and the protection of sacred sites, as well as their ability to practice their religion and traditions, which the federal government had prohibited into the 1970s. Native American tribal communities have fought for their sovereignty for decades. Sovereignty means that tribal governments set the rules and regulations for living within reservation boundaries. Federally recognized tribal groups maintain their own courts to prosecute crimes—with the exception of major crimes, that is, rape, arson, and murder. Native Americans living on their own reservations generally do not need to obey state regulations pertaining to hunting and fishing and do not pay state income or excise taxes, though they are responsible for paying federal income taxes.

Tribal governments also help to create economic opportunities for their people, the subject of Deborah Welch's second volume, *Economic Issues and Development*. In this book, Welch examines the ways in which Native Americans have tried to create employment in businesses, which include ranching, mining, golf resorts, and casinos. She also considers how Native Americans have tried to develop projects within the context of their environmental traditions. As with other elements of their lives, Native Americans try to use their tribal histories and ceremonies to confront the economic challenges of modern life; to prosper by being *both* Native and American, while ensuring the health of Mother Earth.

Limited coverage of Native American life in schools, newspapers, and broadcast media has helped to perpetuate Americans' stereotypical views of Native Americans as either wealthy from gambling or suffering from poverty and alcoholism. The real picture is not so easy to paint and involves more than 560 separate Native American nations within the United States, which includes 4.1 million people who identify themselves as solely or in part Native American. The goal of this series is to explore the many different dimensions of the complex world of today's Native Americans, who are divided by geography, politics, traditions, goals, and even by what they want to be called, Native American or American Indian. Most Native Americans, however, prefer to be identified by their tribal name, for example, Lakota (Sioux), Blackfeet, or Diné (Navajo). And yet Native Americans are some of the most patriotic Americans, in part because their ancestors and relatives have died fighting in the name of freedom, a freedom that has allowed them to be both Native and American. As U.S. Army Sergeant Leonard Gouge of the Oklahoma Muscogee Creek community put it shortly after the September 11 attacks, "By supporting the American way of life, I am preserving the Indian way of life."

Paul Rosier
Villanova, Pennsylvania
March 2005

1

Historical Developments among Native Americans

Some fifty thousand years ago, during the last Ice Age, ancestors of modern Native Americans began their migrations to the Americas. Small bands of hunters traveled from Asia into North America across a land bridge between Siberia and Alaska known today as Beringia. Fleeing the ice, they moved southward, pushed on by other bands that followed; unaware they had entered a new continent. By the time the Ice Age ended and the ocean waters reclaimed the Bering Strait, the migrants had settled throughout North, Central, and South America.

As the centuries passed, these early hunting groups evolved into more advanced and complicated societies, developing economies based on the environments in which they lived. Prior to 5,000 B.C., the cultivation of plants began in Mexico; the knowledge spreading quickly northward. Corn, beans, squash (what Iroquois peoples call

"The Three Sisters"), along with pumpkins, rice, and other staple crops encouraged permanent settlements, particularly east of the Mississippi River. Rich soil accompanied by abundant rainfall led to rapid population growth. In the era before European contact, sometimes known as the Golden Age, Native Americans developed tools and learned to domesticate animals, especially the dog, both as guardians and hunting companions.

In the drier Southwest, cultures such as the Hohokam and Anasazi constructed reservoirs to collect precious rain, digging enormous canals to use that water to irrigate their fields. In the Pacific Northwest, Native Americans relied upon salmon, their principal food source. For those peoples living in the high Great Plains, farming was not possible; they remained primarily hunters, constantly on the go, moving from one site to another in search of food.

Consequently, vastly different environments produced a wide range of economies. In turn, economy served as a primary determinant of social development. Native American populations in the Eastern Woodlands and in California grew large while those in drier climates remained smaller. Early clans and moieties (tribal subdivisions) began to come together as tribes. Along the central Atlantic seashore, some tribes even banded together in mutual self-interest to form powerful alliances, like the Iroquois, the Delaware, and the Powhatan Confederacy, first encountered by the Jamestown colonists in Virginia. By the time the Europeans began to arrive, some three hundred different tribes representing an astounding variety of cultures and traditions lived in what is today the United States. Though well aware of neighboring groups primarily through the development of extensive trade, Native Americans recognized no common identity. They remained divided from one another by language (some three hundred different languages spoken in A.D. 1500), as well as physical appearance. The Cheyennes were quite tall; the Navajos were several inches shorter; some peoples were dark; others very light-skinned. Despite the name Europeans would later use, none were "redskins." Most importantly, they had developed well-established identities based on their tribes by the end of the fifteenth century, unaware of the invasion that was about to begin.

The Arrival of the Europeans

From the beginning, Europeans came for the land and the profit they hoped that land might yield. Gold, silver, and riches beyond belief lay to the west on the far side of the ocean—at least that was the dream that fired European imaginations from the time Homer wrote about the myth of Atlantis beyond the Pillars of Hercules (Gibraltar). Marco Polo's return in the thirteenth century bearing the wealth of the Orient—spices, silk, porcelain, gunpowder, and even spaghetti—only whetted European appetites for more. So in 1492, Columbus set sail, hoping to find a water route to the Indies by traveling west.

Learned Europeans had long accepted the theory that the earth was round, not flat, and by the fifteenth century many supported Copernicus' view of a heliocentric, not geocentric universe. Though his theory was wrong, Copernicus moved science along by proving that the earth orbited around the sun. However, Columbus underestimated the size of the planet. When he arrived in the Bahamas in October 1492, Columbus thought he had reached the Indies he sought and so named the island people he found, Indians.

The race was on to conquer, exploit, and rule. The Spanish may have carried missionaries with them, as did the later French and English invaders, but they also brought guns. The Bible provided window dressing for what was, at its core, a land grab. Europeans called the Western Hemisphere *Vacuum domicillium* (Latin for "empty land"). But the land was far from empty. Population estimates vary widely, ranging from 1.5 million to as high as 4 million Native Americans living in America at the time of contact.

Native Americans did not recognize land ownership, at least not in the European sense. To them, private property, marking an invisible line on the ground dividing what belonged to one person or nation from another made about as much sense as drawing a line in the air to designate individual space. But they recognized spheres of influence and all shared a sense of homeland—*Owenvsv*.

The technical superiority of the European armies determined the outcome of the conflict that followed. First the Spanish and later the English and French used guns, horses, metal, and, most potently of all, disease. Thousands of Native Americans died from smallpox, measles, whooping cough, typhoid, and a host of other illnesses to which they had never been exposed and therefore possessed no immunity. Germs, most often unwittingly taken to the Americas by the invading Europeans, played a major role in weakening its native defenders, making the land all the easier to steal. The invaders sought to destroy culture as well, to convert the Native American to European religion (the Spanish and French brought Catholicism; the English were determined to save heathen souls by imbuing Indian with the New Learning or Protestantism). Even more, they tried to reshape Indian societies into European models. Nationalism, not religion, was a primary motivating force.

But land and the riches on it remained the true goal. For the Spanish, that meant the search for gold and silver throughout South America, Central America, and well into the North American Southwest. Conquistadors soon replaced the first explorers and were led by Hernando Cortez, who destroyed the Aztecs; Francisco Pizarro, who wreaked similar destruction among the Incas; and Francisco Vázquez de Coronado, whose brutality in what is today the U.S. Southwest is still remembered. Spanish rule reached as far north as Colorado. They also established a colony at St. Augustine in Florida.

The French found wealth in beaver pelts. Their invasion

came from the north, down the St. Lawrence River, through the Great Lakes region, and on to the Ohio and Mississippi rivers, which took them into the interior of the continent. Along the riverbanks, the trappers set their snares to catch beaver, the centuries-long fur of choice in Europe for its versatility. Even President Abraham Lincoln's famous stove-pipe hat was made of beaver.

The English, pursuing their settlements along the eastern seaboard of North America, sought gold like the Spanish but with little success. They also participated in the fur trade with willing Native American allies forced to seek English assistance to protect themselves from their enemies who had made similar alliances with the French. Thus, the Haudenosaunee (Iroquois) Confederacy allied with the English because their longtime foes, the Hurons, sided with the French. Similarly, in the South, the Cherokees allied with the English, while the Choctaws traded with the French.

Eventually the English found New World wealth in tobacco, which British king James I called the "stinking weed," deeming it "harmful to the brain" and "dangerous to the lungs." John Rolfe, a leader among the Jamestown colonists, who achieved peace with the powerful Powhatan Confederacy through his marriage to Pocahontas, first developed a hybrid crop and, more importantly, a curing process that would enable tobacco leaves to withstand the salty sea voyage to England. The promised riches of tobacco brought ever-increasing English settlement to Virginia. Other colonies followed—Massachusetts Bay, the Carolinas, Maryland—eventually thirteen in all.

Trade with the British and French

Early Indian efforts at resistance were met with crushing retaliation. The more powerful nations, such as the Haudenosaunees and Cherokees, attempted to coexist, using trade to acquire those metal goods upon which their societies quickly became dependent. Earlier eastern Native Americans had developed some copper mining, usually in shallow pits. They used the metal for fishhooks, knives, and jewelry-making. But the Europeans were more advanced in the uses of metal. They brought guns, needles, cloth, pots, and pans—technology that Native Americans wanted.

At first various Indian tribes traded vegetables; the crops they had developed provided new sources of nutrition previously unknown to Europeans. But the real money lay in fur. Many Native American economies changed as men abandoned farming to secure the furs necessary to trade for European goods. And it was the fur trade that marked European/Indian interaction east of the Mississippi and later to its west, as French trappers began to venture into the Rocky Mountain region.

Burgeoning English populations to the east of the Appalachian Mountains were on the move as well. Led by Daniel Boone and others, these English colonists crossed through the Cumberland Gap, setting up new settlements in modern-day Kentucky and Tennessee, land claimed by many Native Americans—the Shawnees and Cherokees among them. The French regarded all territory west of the Appalachians as their New World colony. On again, off again warfare between France and Great Britain spread to North America in 1754 with the outbreak of the French and Indian War. Most Native Americans fought for the French and indeed continued to fight after France officially surrendered in 1763. Pontiac, an Ottawa leader, formed the first Pan-Indian military movement in American history, as many tribes put aside their long-standing rivalries to join together to resist the common enemy—Great Britain.

To secure the peace, Great Britain offered Pontiac the Proclamation of 1763, which divided the Appalachian Mountains down the center and guaranteed that all lands to the west would be reserved for Native Americans. The Revolutionary War (1776–1783) made that promise meaningless after British general Charles Cornwallis surrendered at Yorktown. Now Americans began flooding across the mountains.

A New Nation; a New Policy

Besieged by other problems in trying to lead a new nation, President George Washington had few resources to protect these would-be settlers from Native Americans determined to defend their lands. His secretary of war, Henry Knox, formulated a policy known as gradualism to deal with Indian nations. The Constitution as well as the Northwest Ordinance of 1787 recognized the sovereignty of those nations, thereby compelling treaty negotiation. Knox sent commissioners to various Indian leaders, using treaty promises, bribes, and threatened military action. Some Native Americans saw no choice but to yield and move farther to the west.

Thomas Jefferson continued the policy of gradualism after he became president in 1801, asking Congress for monies to buy whiskey, intending to use it to befuddle the brains of Indian leaders. Jefferson also began a policy of Americanization, directed exclusively at the Cherokees for whom he had some sympathy. To them he sent missionaries and teachers, including blacksmiths and others; always single men in the hope that they would intermarry with Cherokee women, thereby hastening assimilation into American culture. What followed was a twenty-year period sometimes known as the Cherokee Renaissance, during which the Cherokees adopted American manners of dress, housing, language, and religion. Some even sent their sons to Dartmouth, the college created to educate Indian boys, and transformed their farms into plantations in keeping with the cash-crop economy of their Anglo Southern neighbors (some of the Cherokees even owned slaves).

Louisiana Territory

In 1803, Jefferson acquired Louisiana Territory from France and then sent Meriwether Lewis and William Clark to explore the area. The famous Lewis and Clark expedition identified most of the Great Plains as desert country, land that no white man would ever want. The United States now had a place to send its Indians who stood in the way of expansion and Manifest Destiny—the American belief that God wanted them to have the whole continent from the Atlantic to the Pacific.

In fact, some Native Americans had already begun moving onto the Great Plains. A shift in climate in the mid-eighteenth century, sometimes known as the Little Ice Age, had brought decades worth of rainfall to the plains. As the grass grew, so did the buffalo herds. With guns now in hand (provided by French and English traders) and horses (introduced to the continent by the Spanish), some Native Americans—the Dakotas (Sioux), Cheyennes, and Arapahos, among others, abandoned their farming economies. Pushed by ever-advancing white populations to the east, they ventured onto the plains, developing new societies that relied primarily on the buffalo.

Jefferson and the presidents who followed him saw the desert lands of Louisiana Territory as a solution to their "Indian problem." Forced removals began, climaxing with the election of Andrew Jackson as president in 1828. Land in modern-day Kansas and Oklahoma was declared Indian Territory. The army was used to force Native Americans, most especially the five major tribes of the Southeast—the Cherokee, Choctaw, Chickasaw, Creek, and Seminole—to make the long walk, far from their homes, and begin new lives in Indian Territory. Few escaped. Some Cherokees found refuge deep in the Great Smoky Mountains of North Carolina; others hid in the swamplands. But the majority were force-marched on the journey westward—the Trail of Tears.

Indian Territory

Those who survived the Trail of Tears began new lives in Indian Territory. Many farmed on lands sufficiently arable to permit cultivation. Others began ranching and later turned to leasing grazing lands. They "began river steamer, stage and freight transport systems to service the needs of overland travelers anxious to reach Oregon and California territories as well as Mormon immigrants on their way to Utah and traders traveling between the Missouri River and growing American colonies in Texas."[1] Cherokee, Choctaw, Creek, Chickasaw, and Seminole businesses sprang up to outfit wagon trains, provide supplies, and trade horse and oxen.

Incursion into the West

The onset of American migration westward by covered wagon along the Overland Trail in the 1840s—and most especially after the discovery of gold in California in 1848—brought new incursions against Indian peoples in the West. Gold fever set in as the miners moved from one strike to the next: first in California; then Nevada, finding silver in the Comstock Lode; and on to Colorado, mining gold at a place called Cherry Creek. The Spanish had searched for gold in the Southwest centuries before, finding none. But Americans believed it was still there, and in 1862, General James Carleton ordered his troops into Mescalero Apache and Navajo country. Led by Kit Carson, the army spent two years destroying Navajo orchards and livestock, rounding up as many surviving Navajos as the soldiers could catch, and confining them at Fort Sumner and Bosque Redondo, far from Dinetah, the Navajo homeland between the Four Sacred Mountains.

Other Native Americans were attacked as well, not always by U.S. Army forces, but by self-styled militias who sought to provoke an Indian war and thereby avoid being drafted to serve in the Union Army while the Civil War raged. With the aid of Colorado's territorial governor, John Chivington led a group known as the Colorado Volunteers to attack a Cheyenne and Arapaho village at Sand Creek, located southeast of modern-day Denver. Hundreds of women and children died that day in 1864, while the men were away on a buffalo hunt.

At the end of the Civil War, the regular army returned to the plains, negotiating another Fort Laramie Treaty, reserving once again all lands north of the North Platte River for Native Americans. But gold fever could not be contained. The discovery of gold in Dakota Territory in 1866 brought a new flood of get-rich-quick invaders across the river. Red Cloud's War followed, a small success that forced the miners and the army who had been posted to protect them to leave.

After his election in 1868, President Ulysses S. Grant instituted what became known as "Grant's Peace Policy." Well-intentioned, he put reservations in the care of various Protestant missionary societies, hoping that Native Americans could be transformed into middle-class farmers. But the reservation land in the West was not suitable for farming and gold fever was not cured so easily.

The Black Hills

The Panic of 1873 began a downward spiral of the national economy that would continue for the next thirty years. With little understanding of economics, many Americans blamed the country's depression on inadequate money supplies. Lieutenant Colonel George Armstrong Custer took advantage of this national mood and in 1874, led a force into the Black Hills of South Dakota in search of gold once again. The Black Hills lay well inside those lands reserved to Plains Indians; more importantly the Black Hills are holy, believed by many Sioux and Cheyenne peoples to be the site where God appeared to Sweet Medicine, who carried God's word back to his people.

Black Hills gold was known for its distinctive rosy hue, which became popular for wedding bands in the World War II era and is still often used for high school and college class rings.

Custer was eager to exploit this source of gold, and he took geologists and newspaper reporters along with him on this expedition. But his motives were more self-serving—Custer wanted to start an Indian war, one in which he could demonstrate a heroism that would further his political ambitions, perhaps even propel him into the White House. After all, Washington, William Henry Harrison, Zachary Taylor, Jackson, and Grant had been elected president based on their military reputations.

Custer achieved at least part of his dreams. His 1874 campaign precipitated the "Great Sioux War" of 1875–1877. He would die in that war along with the men he led down into Montana's valley of the Little Big Horn at a place Native Americans called Greasy Grass. Americans would later refer to it as Custer's Last Stand. News of Custer's defeat reached Washington just as Americans were preparing for the Centennial celebration on July 4, 1876. Stunned that "primitive man" could defeat a "modern army" the American public howled for revenge. Politicians began blaming one another, all quickly voting for the necessary funding to send the full might of the United States Army into the West.

Many died on both sides in the battles that followed. Some Native Americans fled to Canada, including a band of Sioux led by Hunkpapa medicine man Sitting Bull. They hid there for a decade until the Canadians, whose Indian policy was no more humane, negotiated Sitting Bull's return. Others were granted small plots of land, reservations on which they were to remain confined.

The Hupas

The West was now open to American settlement and the best land, those areas possessing enough water to make them useful for ranching, was soon taken. Meanwhile, conditions on most reservations declined rapidly. Native Americans struggled to survive because they were crowded onto lands not suitable for farming and made dependent on government agents who delivered food and clothing always inadequate for their needs.

Those people who could live in relative isolation from growing Anglo-American settlements continued to practice traditional economies. One example can be found in the Hupa people of California who, as late as the 1860s, still "lived in an environment of abundance, one that they actively modified with fire to increase its productive potential."[2]

Like many Native Americans, the Hupas practiced a communal economy, dividing labor according to gender. Men hunted and fished; women and children tended crops and saw to the food storage as well. In an effort to avoid encroaching Anglo-American populations, as miners poured into northern California during the Gold Rush, the Hupas abandoned a section of their reservation, at least in part in an unsuccessful effort to avoid the disease the miners unwittingly brought with them. But their way of life could not survive the new Indian policy being devised in Washington, D.C.—Allotment and enforced Americanization.

Allotment and Enforced Americanization

In the late nineteenth century, several reform societies began to form in the East, not unlike the abolitionist organizations a generation earlier. This time, the reformers called for an end to the harsh policies that were killing off Native Americans. Helen Hunt Jackson's 1881 book, *A Century of Dishonor*, roused public opinion with its emotional exposé of reservation conditions and condemnation of U.S. Indian policy. Like so many others, Jackson was not trying to save Indian cultures. The reservations had been created in the first place, at least in part, as places where Native Americans could live in isolation while missionaries and other teachers trained them in the ways of white society. Humane and well intentioned, these reformers remained blinded by their own ethnocentrism—they recognized value in no culture other than their own.

Still, they raised questions for which the American public demanded answers. The reservation system had failed; Native Americans clung to their traditional values. Indeed, among many peoples there existed an almost zealous determination to resist Anglo acculturation. Religious ceremonies continued to be practiced—the Corn Festival and Sun Dance, among others. The Anglo-American nuclear family model (father, mother, children) was rejected in favor of the extended family and old patterns of courtship and marriage were practiced as well. The buffalo long gone, Indian men would turn the cattle delivered by Indian agents out of the corrals, give them a head start, and then hunt them. This spectacle was found to be barbaric by the missionaries, and they demanded that slaughterhouses be built.[3] But episodes like these "beef-hunting days" only gave credence to the reformers' arguments that Native Americans would never learn to live like whites if they remained in isolation on the reservations.

Reaction to the Reservation System

Some, like the Navajos, were allowed to return to their former lands. Others, like the Nez Percé, led by Chief Joseph, attempted escape, only to be hunted down by the U.S. Army and confined to Indian Territory in Oklahoma. New messianic religions began to arise, further outraging the Protestant missionaries. The Ghost Dance first began with the visions of Tavibo, a Paiute man in Nevada. More famously, his son, Wovoka spread his father's message across the Great Plains that all Native Americans should practice love, abstinence from alcohol, and wait for the time when the dead would return and white men disappear. The Ghost Dance cult was a hopeless quest, born out of desperation, but many young people who saw few other options for their lives joined. The apparent frenzy of those rituals, involving all-night dancing, convinced reservation agents that an uprising was imminent among the Sioux, and they called in the U.S. Army. Those Sioux who attempted to flee were

In the 1870s, the Nez Percé, led by Chief Joseph (pictured here), resisted the U.S. government's attempt to force them onto a small reservation in Idaho. After a 1,400-mile march in which they fought U.S. troops for more than three months, the Nez Percé were finally forced to surrender and were removed to lands in eastern Kansas and Oklahoma. Though Chief Joseph spoke against the injustices perpetrated on the Nez Percé by the U.S. government, he was never able to return to his home in the Wallowa Valley of northeastern Oregon; the Nez Percé were instead removed to a reservation in northern Washington.

hunted down by the Seventh Cavalry (Custer's old unit with a score to settle). Massacred at a place called Wounded Knee, their bodies were dumped into a mass grave that may still be visited on the Pine Ridge Reservation in South Dakota.

As the Ghost Dance waned, another religious movement arose in the Southwest. Mexican tribes and some Apaches had used peyote for centuries. Harvested from cactus, the peyote fruit is dried. The resulting "button" produced mild hallucinations among those who indulged. Like the Ghost Dance, the new peyote church incorporated part of Christianity with the old vision quest. Indeed, among some Native Americans, the peyote religion, what Anglos called the Native American Church, is still referred to as the "Jesus Road."[4]

Like the Ghost Dance, peyote represented resistance to U.S. government policies designed to Americanize the Native American. Humanitarians and a growing number of societies in the East demanded action. These outcries for reform fit neatly with western politicians' schemes to destroy the reservations, thus making more land available for non-Indian settlement.

The Dawes Act and a Failing System

In 1887, Congress passed the General Allotment Act, sometimes called the Dawes Act after Senator Henry L. Dawes of Massachusetts who, as chairman of the Senate Committee on Indian Affairs, introduced the bill and served as its primary advocate, pushing it through Congress.

Under the provisions of this new policy, Native Americans would be compelled to embrace the concept of private property ownership. Reservations were surveyed and tribal rolls prepared. An allotment of 160 acres was assigned to each head of household (an Indian man with children). Single Indians over eighteen years of age and orphans less than eighteen received eighty acres. All others were assigned plots of forty acres. The titles to these lands would be held in trust for twenty-five years to protect their Indian owners. The remaining lands, some two-thirds of the reservations, were declared part of the public domain and thus available for purchase by non-Indians, with the proceeds put into a fund for Native American betterment.

Despite outcries from Native Americans and even some of the reformers who realized yet another land grab was about to take place, the legislation passed. President Grover Cleveland condemned the new law as "the hunger and thirst of the white man for the Indian's land. . . ." Native American leaders, such as Lone Wolf (Kiowa), left their reservations, traveling all the way to Washington, D.C., to protest. But they arrived too late; the law had been passed and would remain official Indian policy for nearly the next fifty years.

In 1906, Congress passed the Burke Act, enabling the secretary of the interior to lift the twenty-five-year restriction on sales to free up still more Indian land. At the onset of Allotment in 1887, Indian reservations encompassed approximately 138 million acres. By 1934, only 48 million acres remained in Indian hands, much of it desert country in the Southwest. The funds garnered from the sale of the other two-thirds of reservation land have never been found.

Native Americans continued to resist Allotment. The first allotment assignments on the reservations grouped them together, enabling people to still live in extended families and practice traditional livelihoods—for example, herding sheep from high country in the summers, down to lower altitudes in winter. In response, federal agents began "checker-boarding" the allotment assignments; that is, they would assign 160 acres to an Indian family in the midst of other plots sold to non-Indians. Relatives were thus divided from one another and scattered throughout the former reservations, now surrounded by westerners who usually feared and hated Indians.

Without question, the Dawes Act destroyed the livelihood of many Native Americans, particularly those who lived in Oklahoma and, having lost their original lands in the East, had tried to build new economies in Indian Territory. Now that land was being taken from them as well. Cherokee farmer D.W.C. Duncan testified before a Senate committee in 1906:

Under the old régime, when we were enjoying our vast estate in common here, we all had enough and more than enough to fill up the cup of our enjoyment. . . . While that was the case I had developed a farm of 300 acres up north of town. . . . But when the Dawes Commission sent its survey party around and cut me off up there all but 60 acres, I went to work on that. . . . I had to relinquish every inch of my premises outside of that little 60 acres. What is the result? . . . Away went my crop. . . . Now, that is what has been done to these Cherokees. . . . The government of the United States knows that these allotments of the Indians are not sufficient.[5]

The Americanization policy, touted as an excuse for enacting the General Allotment Act, was applied to Indian children, who began to be rounded up to be separated from their parents and educated in boarding schools in the East. Carlisle Indian School in Pennsylvania and Hampton Institute in Virginia were among the largest. Some Indian parents willingly let their children go, a wrenching decision made because they believed that the next generation's only chance for survival was to become assimilated as the missionaries insisted. These were hard years. By 1900, Native American populations in the United States fell to 250,000 people, all that were left of the millions who had lived throughout America before the Europeans arrived.

Growing charges of incompetence and downright thievery leveled against the Bureau of Indian Affairs (BIA) by both Indians and non-Indians led Secretary of the Interior Hubert Work to appoint a Committee of One Hundred in 1923, charging them with the responsibility of studying and making suggestions about Indian policy. Their report prompted the government to undertake a broader study, for which a private firm, the Institute of Government Research, was contracted to carry out.

Winnebago educator Henry Roe Cloud was one of nine

In 1928, a team of U.S. social scientists released their findings regarding the state of Indian life on reservations. The eight-hundred-page document, known as the Meriam Report, largely blamed Allotment for the deplorable conditions on reservations. The report specifically pointed out the deficiencies in housing, education, and health care. Conditions like those seen in this picture, which is of a toddler on the Navajo Reservation in Arizona, display what reservation life was like in the first half of the twentieth century.

specialists sent by the Institute of Government Research to interview Native Americans and examine reservation conditions over a two-year period, from 1926 to 1928. Their findings were published in an eight-hundred-page document known as the Meriam Report, a truly alarming collection of statistics proving the depth of Indian poverty, as well as the social ills that accompany being poor—inadequate housing, poor education, and widespread illness (especially tuberculosis). For these dire conditions, the investigators blamed BIA mismanagement, particularly that of local reservation agents.

To his credit, President Herbert Hoover tried to make some improvements in Indian policy following his inauguration in 1929. But the stock market crash (only six months after he took the oath of office) and the onset of the Great Depression that followed (in part because of Hoover's ineffectual policies) soon diverted his attention.

Indian Reorganization Act

Despite the disastrous consequences of the Dawes Act, acculturation and assimilation continued as U.S. Indian policy until 1934. Caught up in the Great Depression, Americans elected Franklin Delano Roosevelt to the presidency in 1932. Roosevelt created one of the first "brain trusts"; a group of highly educated and experienced individuals to advise him. One of this group, Harold Ickes, was appointed secretary of the department of the interior, which included the BIA. Ickes named a former social worker, John Collier, to be Commissioner of Indian affairs.

A longtime admirer of Taos Pueblo Indians and a reformer who had achieved some success in protecting Native American lands, Collier set to work with a vengeance to stop the destruction of the reservations and assaults on Indian cultures. One of his first steps was to promote legislation to end the Dawes Act, charging that Allotment had "rendered whole tribes totally landless. It has thrown more than a hundred thousand Indians virtually into the breadline . . ."[6]

Unlike so many policy makers before him, Collier embraced the principle of cultural pluralism—that is, that other cultures have value, equal to that of Anglo-America.

Congress passed his Indian Reorganization Act in 1934. This law ended Allotment. Tribes that accepted the provisions of the IRA were given money to buy back some of the land that had been lost. Collier went further, opening day schools on the reservation so children would no longer be separated from their parents and sent to Eastern boarding schools. Tribal elders were hired along with more traditional teachers. In addition to reading, 'riting, and 'rithmetic—the basic standards of learning—traditional languages and culture were added to the curriculum. New health-care facilities were opened on the reservations and the freedom to practice their traditional religions as they saw fit was once again restored to Native Americans.

Many tribes accepted the benefits of the IRA, reorganizing their government structures and writing constitutions along the models that Collier's agents presented. But those constitutions were based on the Taos society that Collier admired so much. Other Native Americans, proud of their own heritage, resisted Collier's insistence that they adopt alien styles of self-government. Collier listened to those Native American advisors who agreed with him, turning a deaf ear to those who did not. As a result, some tribes rejected the IRA, continuing along a path of resistance that insisted upon the right of self-determination in traditional ways.

Seeking an Identity

The early years of the twentieth century brought both success and failure to Native Americans who were trying to fight for their right to exist. The Supreme Court's *Winters v. United States* decision in 1906 confirmed Blackfeet water rights, vital to their economy in the arid lands of the West. The same court four years earlier, however, denied Kiowa attempts to stop Secretary of Interior Ethan Hitchcock from selling their reservation land in *Lone Wolf v. Hitchcock*. In 1919, Congress passed the Citizenship for World War Veterans Act in an attempt to acknowledge those Indian men who had fought in

Gertrude Bonnin, a Yankton Sioux, was a staunch advocate for Native American rights during the first part of the twentieth century. Though she taught at Carlisle Indian School, she later condemned the school's assimilation policy and sought to unite Native Americans and promote Pan-Indian organizations, such as the Society of American Indians.

World War I. In 1924, Congress extended citizenship to all Native Americans.

By the turn of the twentieth century, new generations of Native American young men and women were coming of age. Educated in the ways of Anglo-American society, they were determined to use its legal system to protect their people. In

1911, the first political Pan-Indian group, the Society of American Indians, mobilized as the only Indian reform organization made up primarily of Native Americans.

But the society floundered after only a little more than a decade, divided by issues of whether or not to cooperate with the Bureau of Indian Affairs, attitudes over the growing peyote church, and, most of all, continuing competition between members of different Indian nations. Gertrude Bonnin (Zitkala-Sa), a Yankton Sioux author rose to become both the society's secretary and editor of its quarterly journal, renamed the *American Indian Magazine*. She also engineered the election of Charles Eastman, a fellow Sioux, as the society's president, clearly feeling that Sioux people should be heard as the voice of Native Americans. Others, notably Chippewa Marie Bottineau Baldwin, one of the first women of color to obtain a law degree, disagreed, as did Thomas Sloan, who believed his Omaha identity to be the equal of any Sioux. Moreover, Sloan defended peyote, putting him in direct opposition to Bonnin, who rejected the Native American Church because it had played no part in Sioux culture.

After Sloan's election as president of the society in 1919, Bonnin broke away, eventually forming her own group, the National Council of American Indians in 1923, with herself as president. Along with her husband, she opposed John Collier's efforts to impose his policies on Native Americans and traveled throughout the West, first to campaign against the Indian Reorganization Act and later to try and organize voter blocs among Native Americans to influence local elections.

Whatever his shortcomings (and they were many), John Collier did succeed in protecting Indian lands from further theft. Moreover, his reservation day schools enabled Native Americans to keep their children with them and their culture intact. Many of the traditional crafts taught to those children (basket-weaving among the Penobscots in Maine, jewelry-making among the Navajos in Arizona and New Mexico, etc.)

would also prove to be important sources of revenue in the years ahead.

During World War II, Collier's policy came under increasing attack. His insistence upon protecting traditional Indian societies had never been accepted by the missionaries who were scandalized that rituals like the Sun Dance could now be performed openly. Necessary wartime rationing of gas and rubber tires made it difficult to keep the school buses running on reservation roads. Caught up in the patriotic fervor of wartime, few Americans supported a federal Indian policy based on cultural pluralism. In the cold war that followed, Collier was even accused of communist sympathies by those determined to return government policy to Americanization.

The enormous debt facing the U.S. government after World War II also played a role in prompting Congress to cut funding to those programs deemed unnecessary. Some members among the Republican-dominated Congress began to demand that the United States resolve its treaty obligations to Native Americans once and for all. Once again the reservations came under attack through a new policy known as Termination.

Termination

In 1946, Congress created the Indian Claims Commission to examine all tribal treaties and find a way to end treaty obligations. A special committee headed by former President Herbert Hoover recommended that all aid promised to Native Americans cease. In addition, the Bureau of Indian Affairs was asked to prepare a list of those tribes whose people were, in their judgment, acculturated and therefore able to live as U.S. citizens without reservation protection.

Not surprisingly, those reservations with rich natural resources were listed as among the first to be taken away. Indian tribes in New York, California, Florida, and Texas were identified for immediate termination in 1953, along with the Flatheads in Montana, Klamaths in Oregon, Menominees in

Wisconsin, Potawatomis in Kansas and Nebraska, and the Turtle Mountain Chippewas of North Dakota. Public Law 280, also passed by Congress in 1953, gave several states jurisdiction over Native American communities.

Soldiers returning from the war wanted to marry, buy a house, and start a family. Lumber companies coveted the rich timber resources of the Menominees and others to feed that burgeoning construction. Many Americans had relocated to the West Coast to work in the wartime aircraft industry and wanted to remain in the 1950s. Thus, California and Oregon Native Americans found themselves slotted for termination. Land values rose in Florida as well; the new holiday destination for tourists in the postwar years. As a result, the Seminole peoples were declared fully ready to live as middle-class Americans, although few of them spoke English and were so poor that most didn't even own a pair of shoes.

Termination, like previous United States Indian policies, was presented to the American public as a benevolent action, freeing Native Americans from "reservation prisons." In fact, it was yet another land grab. Those reservations located on the best land, or possessing valuable natural resources, were identified for immediate termination. Native Americans who lost their land found themselves subject to yet another government relocation program, this one carried out in old buses that took them to cities and dumped them there. As a result, Indian ghettos grew up in Chicago, Illinois; Minneapolis/St. Paul, Minnesota; Denver, Colorado; Los Angeles and San Francisco, California; Phoenix, Arizona; Albuquerque, New Mexico; and a host of other U.S. cities. Today more than 50 percent of all Native Americans live away from the reservation.

Determined to resist this latest onslaught, Native Americans formed yet another reform organization, the National Congress of American Indians, which set out trying to inform the American public about what was really happening and to lobby Congress to protect treaty rights. But a good deal of damage was done throughout the 1950s. Those Native Americans who had developed successful tribal economies,

President Nixon's Self-Determination Policy

Upon taking office in 1969, President Richard Nixon instituted a policy of "New Federalism"; one in which money and political power were diverted from the federal bureaucracy and more toward the local level. Nixon followed this principle when it came to the government's relationship with Native Americans; advocating self-determination among the tribes, and thus bringing an end to the U.S. government's longtime policy of Termination. During his term, the amount of funding for Native American health care doubled, and both the Indian Education Act and the Indian Finance Act were signed into law. What follows is an excerpt from his special message to Congress, in which he promotes a change in federal Indian policy:

> The first Americans—the Indians—are the most deprived and most isolated minority group in our nation. On virtually every scale of measurement—employment, income, education, health—the condition of the Native Americans ranks at the bottom. This condition is the heritage of centuries of injustice. From the time of their first contact with European settlers, the American Indians have been oppressed and brutalized, deprived of their ancestral lands and denied the opportunity to control their own destiny. . . . This then must be the goal of any new national policy toward the Native Americans: to strengthen the Indian's sense of autonomy without threatening his sense of community. We must assure the Indian that he can assume control of his own life without being separated involuntarily from the tribal group. And we must make it clear that Indians can become independent of Federal control without being cut off from Federal concern and Federal support . . . . the Federal government needs Indian energies and Indian leadership if its assistance is to be effective in improving the conditions of Indian life.*

*　Richard M. Nixon, message to Congress on Indian Affairs, July 8, 1970.

such as the Klamaths and the Menominees with their lumber mills, became paupers, reliant upon the state as a result of Termination policies.

Unwilling to take on the responsibility for these new citizens' needs, states that had initially supported Termination began to oppose it in the 1960s. Already, Presidents Kennedy and Johnson were calling for a new approach to Indian policy, one that, as President Johnson stressed, engaged in "partnership, not paternalism." In 1970, President Nixon urged Congress to suspend forced termination. Still, the legislation that enacted that destruction has never been withdrawn. Termination continues as a threat that the federal government can bring to bear when and *if* it sees fit.

Termination is best viewed as part of a continuing government effort to Americanize Indian peoples, to transform them into Anglos—that had been Jefferson's goal, at least for the Cherokees; it was the dream of the missionaries who supported the General Allotment Act. But Native Americans were not so easily defeated. In the aftermath of Termination, Native Americans continued to defend their land and resources, protecting reservations as cultural centers where young people can be taught what it means to be Indian, and developing viable economies to provide jobs for future generations. The chapters that follow will examine some of the fiscal strategies Native Americans have developed to determine their own futures, from tourism, to energy production, to gaming—resisting the efforts made by some states to deny their sovereignty and right to earn a living.

The struggle began in 1492. It continues today. But Native Americans are proven survivors, determined to meet the challenges of a modern economy. For them the goal has always been the same—to protect the homeland. To do that, various Indian nations have turned to a variety of methods to ensure the livelihoods of their people. Not all agree. Considerable debate exists among Indian nations over mining, casinos, and other intrusions of outside businesses in their midst. Those arguments will be examined, as well as the steps taken by Indian nations to assert their right to self-determination.

2

Self-Determination

WHO IS NATIVE AMERICAN?

According to the 2000 U.S. Census, there were 2,475,956 people identified as American Indian and Alaska Native living in the United States, some 0.9 percent of its overall population of 281,421,906.[7] This represents a growing increase over the 1990 census, which listed 1,937,391 people as American Indian and Alaska Native and the 1980 census, which listed those population numbers at 1,478,523.[8] By far the largest nation is the Cherokee with its 400,000 members, followed by the Navajo with approximately 250,000 people. The Sioux are the next largest, followed by the Chippewa, Choctaw, Pueblo, Apache, and Iroquois peoples.

However, census numbers can be misleading. Of the fifty U.S. states, Alaska boasts the largest percentage of Native Americans—15.6 percent, a seemingly statistical anomaly that results from Alaska's overall low numbers of people. Only five states have Indian populations ranging between 4.9 percent and 9.5 percent— Arizona, Montana, North Dakota, Oklahoma, and South Dakota. Washington, Oregon, Nevada, Idaho, Wyoming, Utah, and North Carolina are home to Native Americans representing 1.2 percent to 2.3 percent of their total state populations. These numbers result from the federal government's efforts to survey some 1,081 "specified American Indian and Alaska Native tribes," as well as the large numbers of Native Americans who live in cities today, largely a result of government relocation policies after World War II.[9]

What makes the census takers' job more difficult is the refusal of many people to be pigeonholed into a single racial group or even a single Indian nation. For example: How is the young man with a Cherokee father and a Chippewa mother supposed to choose? And what about a woman born to an Anglo-American father and an Indian mother? Like Tiger Woods, the famous golfer who insists on recognizing both his black and Asian roots, many people quite rightfully wish to embrace their entire heritage. To meet this growing demographic of people of mixed races, the U.S. Census Bureau recognizes fifty-seven possible combinations: Indian and White, Indian and Black, Indian and Asian, and so on, even including one "catch-all" category listed as "American Indian or Alaska Native and some other race."

The growth in Native American populations over the last twenty years must also be considered in the context of the many wannabes—those people who have heard family stories of some distant relative, almost always a grandmother, who was Indian and so want to declare themselves to be Indian also. Only about 1 million of those people who reported to the census takers that they were Native American actually belong to a federally recognized tribe.

In 1846, the Supreme Court declared that for a person to be considered Indian, he or she must have "some" Indian blood and, more importantly, be accepted by a nation or tribe as a member of that group.[10] More than forty years later, the Supreme Court went further, finding that the Cherokee Nation, and by all extension all Indian nations, could establish their own rules regarding who was Indian.[11] This practice continues today and varies widely among the different nations. Among the Onondagas in New York, for example, only the mother's line counts. Children born to an Onondaga man and a non-Onondaga woman cannot be enrolled as members of the tribe. Other Native Americans, like the Arapahos, recognize only the father's line, not the mother's, in determining which offspring will be enrolled as part of the nation. Still others require varying percentages of blood to decide whether or not people may declare themselves to be Native American. The important point is that the decision rests in the hands of the individual Indian nations. Exclusion of children born of mixed marriages seems, at times, to be harsh, but those rules are vital to maintain the cultural integrity of Native American societies.

Life on the Reservation

Reservation populations continued to decline during the decades of Termination policy, as people were forced to move away to seek work. Today, far more Native Americans live off the reservation than on it. This reality does not diminish the importance of the reservation for Native Americans. Far from it—in the twentieth century, Native Americans have transformed these reservations, first established to isolate them from the rest of society, into cultural homelands. The reservations serve as important centers to which all Native Americans can return and bring their children so that they may grow up aware of who they are. As Janet McCloud, an activist born on the Tulalip Reservation, in Washington, once put it, "When all is going crazy . . . our people can come back to the center to find the calming effect; to reconnect with their spiritual self."[12]

Life on the reservation has many benefits, most importantly it is a place where people can live among extended family. But there are challenges as well. The U.S. Census Bureau reported in 1990 that 27 percent of Native American families lived below the poverty level, compared with 10 percent of the population nationwide.[13] While these statistics include those urban Native Americans who often find themselves in low-paying jobs, poverty remains a major challenge for those living on the reservation as well. The loss of the best land, first through Allotment and later under federal reclamation and Termination, accounts for much of this problem. Discrimination against Native Americans who seek employment in towns adjacent to the reservation also contributes to reservation poverty. Even today in places like Thurston County, Nebraska, where more than half of the population is American Indian, none of the county's forty-six employees are tribal members.[14]

Alternatives to Termination

The obvious failure of Termination policy led national leaders in the 1960s to begin to look for new solutions. In 1961, Secretary of the Interior Stuart Udall, acting at the direction of President John F. Kennedy, who had declared his intention to seek justice for Native Americans, appointed a task force on Indian Affairs, with Cherokee leader W.W. Keeler at its head. Like the Meriam Commission had done in 1920s, Keeler's committee visited Native Americans and the reservations. Their final report called for greater Indian control over their own lives and federal policy. Economic development, they stressed, was crucial. Two other nationwide studies, one by the Commission on Rights, Liberties and Representatives of the American Indian, similarly concluded that Termination had failed. The U.S. Commission on Civil Rights agreed, offering statistics on employment discrimination applied against Native Americans.

Several other reports followed. The Coleman Report, released in 1966, harshly criticized American Indian policy, charging that centuries of Americanization had created a marginal people of confused identity. Discrimination in the schools had produced a generation suffering "more stigma and self-hatred than any other ethnic group." The Coleman Report led to an ongoing Senate investigation that formed a special subcommittee on Indian education. After a series of hearings, it recommended that Native American parents should be allowed to form their own school boards to oversee their children's education.

A White House Commission on Indian health undertook similar studies. Their findings were so dismal that those reports have never been released. All this increased federal attention was having little effect on the day-to-day lives of Native Americans, leading Wendell Chino, governor of the Mescalero Apaches, to complain, "We Indians have been studied to death by task forces."[15]

The Red Power Movement

Frustration over the federal government's repeated failure to fulfill its trustee responsibilities guaranteed in countless treaties led to the onset of new Native American activism in the 1960s and 1970s, primarily carried out by young Native Americans. Cherokee scholar/activist Robert K. Thomas predicted, "As I look around at the Indian situation, it looks like one big seething cauldron about ready to explode."[16] In 1960, a group of primarily college students broke off from the National Congress of American Indians to form their own organization, the National Indian Youth Council, which started its own newspaper, *ABC* (*Americans Before Columbus*). By the end of the decade, another group had formed, the American Indian Movement, or AIM.

Borrowing heavily from the strategies developed by the Black Civil Rights Movement of that same era, the "Red Power" movement staged demonstrations designed to capture maximum television coverage: the 1969 takeover of Alcatraz Island and the closed prison facilities there, the 1970 protest atop

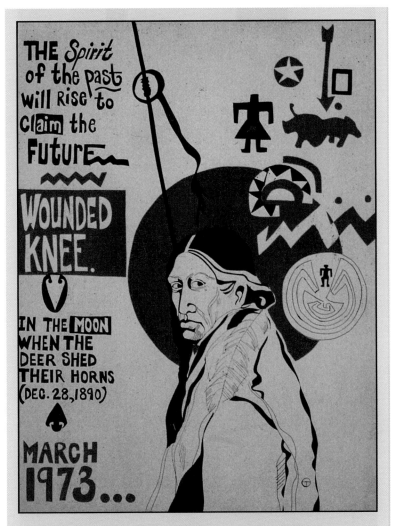

THE *Spirit* of the past will Rise to Claim the FuturE

WOUNDED KNEE.

IN THE MOON WHEN THE DEER SHED THEIR HORNS (DEC. 28, 1890)

MARCH 1973...

During the early 1970s, the "Red Power" movement utilized a series of public demonstrations to draw attention to the plight of Native Americans. One such demonstration was the occupation of the community church and general store at Wounded Knee Creek, South Dakota, during the spring of 1973. The occupation turned into a seventy-day siege when Native Americans demanded that past treaties be honored, and that both the BIA and the Pine Ridge government be investigated for wrongdoings. This poster commemorates the 1890 massacre at Wounded Knee and the continuing struggle for Native American equality.

Mount Rushmore, the 1972 automobile caravan to Washington, D.C., called the Trail of Broken Treaties, and perhaps most famously, the 1973 occupation of the community church and general store at Wounded Knee, South Dakota, site of the massacre of Sioux Indians in 1890. These and other activities raised the sympathies and a certain amount of alarm among the non-Native American public, most of whom preferred to think of Indians, when they thought of them at all, as "noble savages," a term first coined by the Enlightenment writer, Rousseau, and firmly planted in American minds by Hollywood.

But national attention did little to alleviate the ongoing poverty on the reservations, where many Native Americans decided to take matters into their own hands rather than wait for long-promised, but slow in coming, federal assistance. In Washington State, the Medicine Creek Treaty of 1854 had guaranteed Native Americans fishing rights both on and off the reservation. State game wardens ignored that treaty, prodded into action by commercial canneries and so-called sportsmen, and began arresting Native American fishermen in a series of carefully staged raids. A series of "fish-ins" followed, orchestrated in large part by Janet McCloud on the Nisqually River between Olympia and Tacoma, as well as Puget Sound and the Columbia River. On October 13, 1965, stage agents surrounded a fish-in of about fifty people, dispersing the group with clubs. McCloud was among those charged with resisting arrest and she was taken to prison, where she began a fast in protest. In the end she was acquitted because the riot on the Nisqually that day was caught on tape, which provided visual evidence that Indians had not started the fight. Civil Rights activist Dick Gregory and even Marlon Brando joined the fish-in struggle; Gregory was sent to jail for ninety days, where he also fasted in protest.[17]

Taking Action

Just as Native Americans had learned to use the media, so too were they becoming well-acquainted with the U.S. legal system.

Janet McCloud and "Fish-ins"

Janet Renecker was born on the Tulalip Reservation in Washington State on March 30, 1934, and was a descendent of Suquamish chief Seattle's family. Raised Catholic, Renecker did not grow up following her tribe's customs and traditions. She married Don McCloud, a Nisqually tribal fisherman, in the early 1950s, and they began raising a family near the Nisqually Reservation in Yelm, Washington. However, her simple life would change dramatically in the early 1960s.

The commercial fishing industry had been an integral part of the Seattle area economy, but by the 1960s, the number of salmon and steelhead in the Nisqually and Puyallup rivers had been greatly reduced by overfishing. The State of Washington set out to stop local Indian tribes from fishing these rivers, so that they could save the fish for the commercial fishermen. Despite the fact that the Indian tribes had signed treaties with the federal government more than one hundred years before, the Washington State Supreme Court upheld injunctions that allowed the state to regulate tribal fisheries. As a result of this injustice, McCloud and her husband, Don, formed an activist group known as the Survival of American Indians Association. The group began to participate in "fish-ins," where they would toss their traditional fishing nets into the rivers in protest. Fish-ins drew worldwide attention and even actor Marlon Brando participated in this unique form of protest. On one such fish-in, Janet McCloud was arrested, and what follows is an account by her daughter, Laura, describing her mother's court testimony:

> She told how she felt when she realized that the game wardens were going to ram our boat and how she felt when she realized these men meant business with their 7-celled flashlights, billy clubs, and brass knuckles. My two little brothers were in that boat when it was rammed, the youngest was 7 and could not swim. Besides, once you get tangled in nylon mesh it is very easy to drown. While she was telling this story, we could tell she was trying very hard to keep from crying, but this did not help because she started to. And every Indian in that courtroom that was there that horrible day started to remember the fear and anger that they had felt that day. . . .*

*   Peter Nabokov, *Native American Testimony* (New York: Penguin/Putnam, Inc., 1999), 364.

Native Americans in Washington State had been guaranteed fishing rights on the Nisqually and Puyallup rivers since signing the Medicine Creek Treaty with the U.S. government in 1854. However, during the 1950s and '60s, commercial fishermen over-fished the two rivers and the State of Washington began a policy of banning Native Americans from using traditional methods of catching fish. This 1966 "fish-in" on the Nisqually River shows a group of Native Americans pulling in a catch of salmon.

In 1974, a suit brought to the U.S. District Court in Washington State resulted in a decision by judge George Boldt that Indians were entitled to catch up to 50 percent of the salmon (indeed all fish) returning to "the usual and accustomed places designated by the treaties of the 1850s."[18]

What followed was even greater violence—outraged non-Indians burned Boldt in effigy. In the end, however, both the sportsmen and the commercial canneries were compelled to negotiate with Native Americans to protect the salmon runs, each taking a designated and limited share designed to safeguard continued salmon stock in the rivers.

LaDonna Harris

While resistance grew in reservation communities, other Native Americans sought help more directly from the federal government. One of the best examples of an Indian leader who has used federal policies to promote economic development is LaDonna Harris. A Comanche, Harris was born in 1931 near Lawton, Oklahoma. Like many women of her generation, she expected to spend her life as a wife and mother. Her husband's election to the Oklahoma state senate in 1952 thrust the couple into politics. A liberal reformer, Fred Harris wrote the legislation to create the Oklahoma Human Rights Commission in 1958 to stop discrimination and create jobs for peoples of all colors, including Native Americans.

In 1964, Fred Harris ran as the Democratic Party's candidate for the U.S. Senate seat and won—an unexpected victory. The Harris family found itself moving to Washington, D.C., using a house in McLean, Virginia, not far from the Robert F. Kennedy family with whom they grew close. Robert Kennedy introduced Fred and LaDonna Harris to the "movers and shakers" among the Democratic Party during the 1960s, including Hubert Humphrey, Walter Mondale, and Stuart Udall, then secretary of the interior. Indeed, LaDonna Harris became close friends with Udall's wife, Lee, and later traveled with Joan Mondale visiting Indian reservations.[19] Most significantly, Robert Kennedy introduced LaDonna Harris to his sister, Eunice Kennedy Shriver, and her husband, Sargeant Shriver, who had been appointed to run the Office of Economic Opportunity (OEO).

Spearheading the drive in the Johnson Administration's war on poverty, the OEO offered opportunities desperately needed on Indian reservations—to promote education and job training. With her husband's support, LaDonna Harris first galvanized an Oklahoma community action group into getting underway in 1965. Other meetings followed, organized in part by LaDonna Harris' mass-mailing campaign and culminating in the organization of Oklahomans for Indian Opportunity (OIO) later that year, with Harris acting as president of the executive board.

With clerical support provided by the Southwest Center for Human Relations, directed by John B. O'Hara at the University of Oklahoma, the OIO amassed alarming statistics about Oklahoma's Native Americans. For many of them, their formal education stopped at about grade 5 or 6, permanently handicapping their ability to find jobs in a twentieth-century economy. Indian earnings averaged about half that of non-Indian residents.

Using the grant funds made available by the OEO, LaDonna Harris and the OIO were able to organize a number of projects: opening job referral centers in Indian communities, providing aid in the form of food and clothing when needed, and working with tribal governments to establish leadership programs. At the same time, Harris drew upon her Washington connections to invite those with real power to come to Indian country and see the economic hardships. One of those visitors was Robert F. Kennedy, who wowed a crowd of Indian young people with his opening comment, "I'd like to be an Indian."[20] To generations who had endured the taunts of their classmates who used Indian as a derisive term, that simple statement provided a much-needed affirmation.

In 1967, Fred and LaDonna Harris were instrumental in persuading President Lyndon Johnson to create the National Council for Indian Opportunity, which promoted the nationwide emphasis on education and job training espoused by the OIO. This council proved to be short-lived. After Richard Nixon was elected president in 1968, he appointed his vice-president, Spiro Agnew, to chair the agency. Agnew effectively killed it by refusing to call any meetings.

Three years later, LaDonna Harris created the Americans for Indian Opportunity, attracting a number of Indian notables to its board of directors, including the poet N. Scott Momaday, reformer Ada Deer, and Peterson Zah, later chairman of the Navajo Nation. The political winds in Washington, D.C., had obviously shifted drastically, resulting in significant cuts for all domestic programs, including the OEO. The Americans for Indian Opportunity felt it could gain support from private foundations. It fell to LaDonna Harris to do much of the grant writing, a formidable task that took up most of her time, but in the end, she was successful, gaining funds to promote job training on Indian reservations nationwide and assisting tribal governments in dealing with federal bureaucracy.

LaDonna Harris' work in making federal officials aware of the damage inflicted by past Indian policies, as well as the notoriety achieved by groups like AIM, prodded Congress into action. The result was the 1972 passage of the Indian Education Act, which provided funding for public-school education for Native American children. The Indian Self-Determination and Educational Assistance Act, which transferred administration of federal programs to tribal authorities, followed this act in 1975. Equally important was the 1974 Indian Financing Act that guaranteed grants and loans to Indian nations to encourage economic development; this resulted in the creation of the Indian Business Development Program. In 1978, Congress passed the Indian Religious Freedom Act and the Indian Civil Rights Act.

Despite this flurry of legislation in the 1970s, all ostensibly enacted to promote Indian self-determination, many Native Americans remained wary. These are a people who had seen many federal promises over the centuries. Few had been kept and others came with an ulterior motive—like the Dawes Act. True self-determination meant that Native Americans would continue to find the means to ensure their survival on their own terms. Tribal economic viability was the key to cultural endurance. In his 1971 inaugural address, Navajo Tribal Chairman Peter MacDonald laid out that strategy:

First, what is rightfully ours, we must protect; what is rightfully due us we must claim. Second, what we depend on from others, we must replace with the labor of our own hands, and the skills of our own people. Third, what we do not have, we must bring into being. We must create for ourselves.[21]

3

Tourism

- ◇ - ◇ - ◇ -

One of the means Native Americans first used to become economically self-sufficient was through the promotion of tourism. Native Americans—not individual Indian nations or societies about which most people have little understanding and probably care even less—have long fascinated Americans. They are colorful relics of U.S. history, or at least the version of it presented through novels and cinema. What has always surprised and dismayed Native Americans is the American assumption of a right to use and exploit their images at will. Witness the use of logos and mascots from the Cigar Store Indian figure to sports teams like the Atlanta Braves and Washington Redskins to selling Red Man Chewing Tobacco, with the requisite image of a Plains Indian war chief on the packaging.

During the first half of the twentieth century, dirt roads like this one were the only way tourists could travel through the Hopi and Navajo reservations of northern Arizona. However, travel by automobile began to become easier in the decades following World War II, with the construction of such highways as Interstate 40, which made Monument Valley and the Grand Canyon accessible to many tourists.

A New Era

The dawn of the twentieth century brought about the invention of the automobile, a new toy with which Americans quickly fell in love. Of course, cars are useless without roads and so the nation began building them, usually just two-lane byways in the 1920s. Highway construction meant jobs and so members of Congress set about passing the necessary appropriations, fighting for their own states' fair share of the money.

Virginia was one of the first to take advantage of this new demand for roads. Construction of the Skyline Drive began during the 1920s and was completed by the Civilian Conservation Corps (CCC) during President Roosevelt's New

Deal in the 1930s. Anxious to put Americans to work during the Great Depression, President Roosevelt's administration designed a number of employment programs—including the Works Progress Administration (WPA) and the Tennessee Valley Authority (TVA)—to bring hydro-electrical power to the Smoky Mountain regions of eastern Tennessee and western North Carolina. As the Depression continued throughout the 1930s, the CCC expanded its Skyline Drive construction into the Blue Ridge Parkway, a winding scenic road that extends through the Appalachian Mountains from Front Royal, Virginia, to the southern highlands of North Carolina.

The Cherokees

The Blue Ridge Parkway took travelers close to the Qualla Boundary, home to the Eastern Band of Cherokee peoples—those who had escaped President Jackson's removal policies in the 1830s. Hidden deep in the Smoky Mountains, the Cherokees had continued to live, largely isolated from non-Indian society. They farmed as their ancestors had done for thousands of years before contact, supplementing their diets with fish, deer, and wild turkeys. But as the roads reached them, the Cherokees found new and much-needed sources of income.

The town of Cherokee, North Carolina, began building stores to meet the expectations of tourists; there they sold toys, mostly little black bears, tom-tom drums, and moccasins. The white tourists wanted to see Native Americans like those John Wayne had fought in the movies. So the Cherokees sold feathered headdresses, more appropriate to Plains people, and it quickly became a joke among them—if whites were silly enough to buy them, the Cherokees would sell them. The tourists came looking for Pocahontas and the Cherokees obliged them—even selling squaw dolls (complete with a papoose on her back).

President Eisenhower's determination to build an interstate highway system similar to Germany's autobahn, which he had admired during World War II, brought even more tourists to Cherokee after the Federal Aid Highway Act became law in 1956. And the Eastern Band was ready for them. One of the major attractions they developed was the outdoor drama, *Unto These Hills*, first produced in 1949 and set in a hillside arena surrounded by the beautiful Smoky Mountains. The drama begins at sunset after the audience has had a chance to watch the mists roll in over the peaks, which provide nature's backdrop to the stage. A cast of more than one hundred tells the story of the Cherokees from 1540 through the Trail of Tears in 1838.

As tourist revenues grew, the Cherokees opened Oconaluftee Indian village, a replica of an eighteenth-century Cherokee community complete with guides to demonstrate basket-weaving, wood-carving, finger-weaving, and other traditional Cherokee arts. Today there are a host of sites in and around Cherokee, including the Museum of the Cherokee Indian. The Museum has recently installed a new exhibit using sophisticated computer imagery to tell the fifteen-thousand-year story of the Cherokee (Tsalagi) people.[22]

Tourism on the Qualla is a genuine success story. The Eastern Band of Cherokee (EBC) has built a viable economy based on the thousands of visitors who come every year. Problems remain, of course. Few tourists venture beyond the towns into the backcountry of these mountains nor would they be particularly welcome to do so. Many elderly people still live simple lives in these hills, large numbers of whom must deal with Type II diabetes. This disease, the scourge of most Native Americans, seems especially prevalent among the Cherokees.

Still, the Cherokees have used tourism not only to increase tribal revenues but, more importantly, as an avenue to preserving culture. Future generations, both Indian and non-Indian, will be taught traditional Tsalagi values in the museums and cultural centers, which tourist dollars enabled the EBC to build.

The Penobscots

Other Native Americans explored different strategies to bring in tourist revenues. One of the most energetic proponents of the Penobscot peoples was Lucy Nicolar. In the early twentieth century, Nicolar, well known on the vaudeville entertainment circuit as Princess Watahwaso, returned home to Indian Island, the Penobscot Reservation in Maine. There she helped organize a series of pageants that brought thousands of tourists every summer. Even more importantly, those events helped "to renew old times and customs so the ways of our fathers will not be forgotten by our children."[23] Like the Cherokees in their early tourism efforts, Nicolar was not particular about the means she used to attract tourists. At one point, she had a two-story tepee built and painted white and red so it would be easily visible from the mainland. Curious travelers flocked to the site where Nicolar hired Penobscot people, mostly women, to weave baskets to sell to these tourists along with moccasins, rattles, and toy canoes—the usual inventory Americans wanted to purchase in the reservation shops. Like the Cherokees, the Penobscots played to those expectations. Some may criticize this as a betrayal of culture, but in the Depression era, dollars were desperately needed.

Indian Arts and Crafts Board Act

Preserving culture as well as finding some means of bringing much-needed money to tribes was the goal of John Collier, commissioner of Indian affairs during the Roosevelt administration. To accomplish his goals, Collier pushed Congress to pass the Indian Arts and Crafts Board Act in 1935.[24]

The five-person board was charged with finding new ways to help Native American economic development through arts and crafts industries. They provided the marketing expertise, offering technical advice, and even created federal trademarks to guarantee the authenticity of Native American products. This law made it a federal offense for non-Indians to try and sell crafts as genuine articles.

The Navajos and Hopis

Most Native Americans lived in the West on isolated reservations not accessible by roads, making it difficult for tourists and the dollars they brought to reach those reservations. To be sure, Native American crafts had long been prized. In the late nineteenth and early twentieth centuries, growing numbers of trading posts, almost always operated by non-Indians, had grown up on the Navajo Reservation. The traders soon recognized the beauty and marketability of Navajo rugs and jewelry. Importing vertical looms adopted from the Pueblo people, the traders encouraged Navajo women to weave large rugs that the traders then sold for incredible profits to Eastern buyers. Many Navajo men were skilled silversmiths, often using silver dollars to create belt buckles, bracelets, and other jewelry. By the turn of the twentieth century, it had become commonplace to use turquoise as well as silver. Easily available because it was mined nearby, turquoise became a distinctive tribal look, both for the Navajos and for non-Indians, who found the blue stones in their silver settings to be beautiful.[25]

However, most Navajos did not speak English. They relied on the traders to market their wares, usually to markets east of the Mississippi. Thus, while the traders made a hefty profit, Navajo people did not benefit at the same rate and these "home industries" did not increase tourism. As interstate travel became more accessible in the decades following World War II, tourists have begun to visit the Navajo Reservation. Many pass through Monument Valley on their way to the Grand Canyon and other popular destinations. The roadsides are dotted with Navajo families, many of whom simply pull a car off, spread out a blanket, and display their wares. Most tourists visiting the Southwest today are well aware of the incredible bargains to be found in buying from these individual Navajo people. And at least this way, the full profits go to the artisans.

Every tourist, it seems, has a camera. In addition to buying

Navajo jewelry stands like this one near the Grand Canyon dot the roadsides of north-central Arizona. Skilled Navajo artisans offer jewelry, much of which is made of turquoise and silver, but also pottery and rugs to tourists.

jewelry, these shutterbugs start snapping away as soon as they leave their cars. Some, all too few it often seems, possess the courtesy to ask permission first. Long accustomed to tourist curiosity, many Navajos smile, nod, and respond: "$5.00." They have, indeed, become savvy businesspeople and have developed a tolerance for rudeness as well—most of the time. This author remembers one occasion where a tourist who had been taking pictures of some Navajo children was chased back to her car by an irate grandmother who was providing an additional lesson in some well-chosen Navajo words.

The work of scholars like Peter Iverson, who has written many studies of the Navajo Nation, and the popular novels of Tony Hillerman, who sets his Joe Leaphorn-Jim Chee mysteries among the Navajos, have, no doubt, prompted an increase in tourism in recent years.

Not far from the Navajos live the Hopi and Pueblo peoples. Maria Montoya Martinez of the San Ildefonso Pueblo of northern New Mexico became the most famous Indian potter in the country. Along with her husband, Julian, she crafted intricately decorated black on black pottery that catapulted her to national attention in the 1920s. In keeping with Pueblo tradition, Maria shared her skills with other Pueblos who came to her for instruction. The resulting profits helped many families survive during the lean years of the 1930s.

Virginia Tribes

Many tribes today attempt to cash in on tourism dollars in an effort to promote economic self-sufficiency. This includes both federally recognized tribes and other people. In Virginia, for example, there exist eight Indian tribes recognized by the state but not by the Bureau of Indian Affairs. They are small groups of people, some numbering less than one hundred—all who are left of the once-powerful Powhatan Confederacy: Monacan, Manahoac, Susquehanna, and Rechahecrian peoples who numbered in the tens of thousands when the English landed at Jamestown in 1607. But these descendents celebrate their Indian heritage proudly. The Chickahominys, who live midway between Richmond and Williamsburg, host powwows and a fall festival every year, using the proceeds to build a tribal center for the community. Similarly, the Rappahannocks have begun building a tribal museum.

Non-Indians

Of course, non-Native Americans have tried to use some link to Indian history to attract tourist dollars as well. In 2004, North Little Rock, Arkansas, emphasized its role as a "significant station along the Trail of Tears" as part of its centennial celebration. Some thirty to forty thousand Native Americans

Maria Montoya Martinez, pictured here on the right in a 1934 photo, was renowned for reviving the black-ware pottery technique of the ancient Pueblos. Maria and her husband, Julian, were natives of the San Ildefonso Pueblo of northern New Mexico, which is known for its high iron content that turns clay black when fired. The Martinez's work was so admired that they were asked to display some of their pottery at both the 1904 and 1934 World's Fairs.

passed through there during the 1830s and 1840s on their way to forced relocation in Indian Territory.[26] Countless other examples exist of people who lay some claim to a distant Indian ancestor and host events to celebrate that culture.[27]

This assumption by all Americans that they have the right to lay claim to Indian identity as part of their own cultural heritage lies at the core of the reason why tourism has failed to become a significant income source for most reservations. The majority of Americans are most comfortable celebrating Native American societies from afar—for example, on a movie screen.

The Reservation Economy

Urban Native Americans have long grown accustomed to their minority status, or as a friend of this author once put it, she's usually "the only whole wheat skin in a room full of wonder bread." Reverse the racial percentages and many non-Indians find themselves a little ill at ease at being the minority. They have seen too many John Wayne movies and the legend of Custer dies hard.

Some visitors to the reservation express their disappointment at being there. One example is a man who asked if the phone poles he saw were really necessary. Didn't they interrupt "the Indians' psychic/spiritual connection to the earth?" He never asked "Indians whether they appreciated the convenience of finally being able to call friends, government agencies, and doctors."[28] People come to see feathers and totem poles, not real Native Americans.

Many of the reservations continue to be too isolated for both tourism and arts and crafts to be a viable source of income. However, in some cases tourism has proven a success. In the lean years of the Depression, it brought in a few dollars. Today, it has provided funds to establish tribal museums and cultural centers. And the growth of interest in Native American art in the twentieth century helped launch the careers of talented artists like painter Fred Beaver (Creek), Patrick DesJarlait (Asnishinaabe), Timothy Begay (Navajo), and Arnold Jacobs (Onondaga).[29] Indeed, selling supposedly genuine Native American crafts has become a thriving industry among many non-Indians who combine traditional Native American art forms with New Age mysticism. Interested readers may check internet auction sites for evidence of the explosion in the availability of these items. Some Native American groups try to protect their art through websites that promote Indian artists and their work.[30]

In addition to the Eastern Band of Cherokees in North Carolina, other tribes have developed hotels and other attractions to draw in visitors, including the Warm Springs Reservation in Oregon and the Mescaleros of New Mexico. The hotels, roadside stands, and cultural museums are easily accessible along major thoroughfares. Many visitors traveling through northern Arizona on their way to the Hopi Mesas or other sites have stopped for a Tuba City Taco, made famous by its enormity. Scenic pull-offs along these highways are usually crowded with Navajo families selling their homemade goods on blankets spread beneath tarps, offering some shade against the hot Arizona sun.

On these public areas of the reservation, visitors are welcome. Although tourists may travel anywhere on the reservations, poor roads usually inhibit all but the most hearty adventurers, some of whom put too much faith in their rental car dealers' assurances about what four-wheel drive vehicles can do. This author has picked up more than one stranded traveler who foolishly went into Navajo and Hopi backcountry without a full tank of gas and extra water for the radiator.[31]

Similar problems exist on the Qualla Boundary among the Eastern Band of Cherokees. Most tourists use U.S. Route 74 to reach Cherokee and then return to Interstate 40, but there are always a few who wander out onto the winding mountain roads looking for "real" Cherokees. The people who live in these hills do not appreciate the intrusion. A case in point is an elderly woman whom everyone calls Aunt Maggie. Widowed many years ago, she lives in a small frame house accessible only by a footbridge that crosses a creek. She has no driveway, only a gravel pull-off by the side of the road near the footbridge. Aunt Maggie's front yard is usually crowded with grandchildren who have unfortunately grown accustomed to hearing the sound of car brakes as some tourist stops in the middle of the road to step out and take photographs of her grandchildren.

Undoubtedly, these tourists mean no harm. In fact most of them are usually quite friendly, hoping for the chance to talk to "real" Indians—the oft-heard phrase. But Native Americans value their privacy like everyone else. Moreover, they have five hundred years of reasons not to trust. No Cherokee is going to invite a stranger into his or her home for kanuchi or some other tribal delicacy.[32]

In short, tourists are welcome—in tribal cultural centers, restaurants, shops, theaters, and other public facilities on the reservation. This is the part of Indian life tribal governments want visitors to see. In the museums and cultural centers, tourists can learn about Native American societies. The shop-keepers are "real" Indians and are, of course, willing to talk to their customers.

Many tourists simply do not understand what they see on the rest of the reservation. Sociologists—"drunk counters" as some Native Americans call them—blotted their copybooks long ago by describing Native American land as desolate and depressing. In the opening lines of his book, *American Indians and Federal Aid*, sociologist Alan L. Sorkin wrote, "An Indian reservation can be characterized as an open-air slum. It has a feeling of emptiness and isolation. There are miles and miles of dirt or gravel roads without any signs of human life."[33]

What Sorkin did not see was the warmth of the Indian family, the social and economic safety net that comes with being surrounded by one's relatives and belonging to a community that cares for all its members. He wrote instead about poverty and blamed Indians for most of it.

Today many Indian nations hope that the museums and other annual cultural events, such as powwows, will remind their children of the unique value of their identity as Indians and enable other non-Indians to develop greater understanding. But for the majority of Indian nations, tourism alone cannot bring about the fiscal self-sufficiency for the reservations to continue to exist. To achieve that goal, other means have to be sought.

4

Energy Development

- ◇ · ◇ · ◇ -

THE THEFT OF NATIVE AMERICAN LAND AND RESOURCES

Government reservation policy throughout the nineteenth century had been devoted to relocating Native Americans to plots of land no one else wanted. For the most part, this meant arid areas in the West unsuitable for farming—those regions on the Northern Plains first designated by the Lewis and Clark Expedition as "the Great American Desert." Some Indian nations were luckier than others. The Navajos, for example, were allowed to return to their homeland and today live on the largest reservation in the United States, comprising some thirty-two thousand square miles in Arizona, New Mexico, southern Utah, and southern Colorado. But the land is desert, suitable, in the eyes of federal policy makers, only for the Navajos to eek out a living, largely through sheep grazing. Other Native Americans, like the Cherokees, on whose land gold was found at Dahlonega in the early nineteenth century, were forcibly removed to Indian Territory, originally an area encompassing most of present-day Kansas and Oklahoma.

Ironically, it is on these so-called barren lands that many of the mineral riches needed in the twentieth and twenty-first centuries are found. Americans' love affair with the automobile and their reliance on all forms of mass transportation, particularly the airplane, calls for large supplies of oil and petroleum, much the same as it did during the era of industrial growth in the early twentieth century. World War I made clear that both defense and the United States' emerging role as the commercial/industrial leader of the world required fuel—coal, oil, and natural gas—for its ships, airplanes, cars, homes, and factories. After World War II and the development of atomic energy, uranium joined that list of needed energy resources, a sizeable amount of which was to be found on reservation lands. It is estimated that "one-third of all western low-sulpher coal, one-fifth of the country's reserves of oil and natural gas, and over half the nation's uranium deposits," lie beneath reservation soil.[34]

Tragedy in Oklahoma

The theft of American Indian energy resources in the twentieth century began in Oklahoma after it was discovered that Native Americans were living on enormous petroleum reserves. In 1908, Congress, bowing to pressure from Oklahoma, had removed allotment restrictions and transferred all probate decisions and guardianship responsibilities from the Indian Office to Oklahoma county courts. Those courts declared all Indian adults and some sixty thousand children incompetent to manage their own affairs and appointed Anglo guardians and attorneys to supervise their property. Unconscionable men scrambled for these lucrative appointments. At stake were considerable profits to be made through the sale of oil, as well as timber, led, coal, and zinc, and valuable agricultural and grazing leases.[35] In 1914, the commissioner of Indian affairs

Oil fields such as Three Sands, just south of Tonkawa, Oklahoma, were set up on Indian reservation lands during the first couple of decades of the twentieth century. In 1921, Three Sands produced more than 60 million barrels of oil and became known as the "billion dollar spot," but none of the profits went to Native Americans.

attempted to stem the tide of graft, or unfair gains, by drawing up rules of procedure for the probate courts. But in 1923, the state court returned full probate powers to the county courts, a move that prompted the American Indian Rights Association (IRA) to launch an investigation—sending a team to Oklahoma that included Yankton Sioux writer and activist Gertrude Bonnin.

Bonnin, along with Matthew K. Sniffen and Charles H. Fabens published their findings the following year in a thirty-nine-page pamphlet entitled *Oklahoma's Poor Rich Indians: An Orgy of Graft and Exploitation of the Five Civilized Tribes, Legal Robbery*. Their statistics were horrifying, proving that lawyers and court-appointed guardians were taking up to 70 percent of Indian estates as "administrative costs" while their Indian charges died of malnourishment or untreated illnesses. One attorney received $35,000 from a ward's estate even though the lawyer had done nothing; he had never even appeared in court. The IRA publication brought charges of kidnapping and even murder against some of the guardians.

The American Indian Defense Association, along with the General Federation of Women's Clubs, joined the IRA in demanding a Congressional investigation into the activities of Oklahoma's probate courts. During the investigation, which got underway in November 1924, attorneys representing oil company interests and county officials succeeded in turning the inquiry into a witch-hunt, exposing those people who had cooperated with Bonnin, Fabens, and Sniffen. Predictably the subcommittee exonerated the county courts, declaring them to be lily-white. But the truth was obvious. Newspaper editors in Oklahoma and elsewhere in the country denounced the hearings as a sham. The Oklahoma Bar Association chastised its members who had gotten rich on the bodies of Native Americans. In the face of growing public pressure, the Oklahoma legislature passed the Frye Bill, placing maximum limits on the fees attorneys and guardians could collect from Indian wards. But much of the damage had already been done.

In 1938, Congress passed the Omnibus Tribal Leasing Act, which empowered the Department of Interior to negotiate and approve all leases between Indian tribes and mining companies. The law was intended to enable the federal government to fulfill its trustee obligations and protect Native Americans from state and corporate greed. In reality, however, the Department

A Voice for Native Americans

Gertrude Bonnin, also known as Zitkala-Sa, was born in South Dakota in 1876 and was a member of the Yankton Sioux Nation and a political activist. When she was eight, she was sent to a mission school in Indiana, and later attended college in that state and studied music in Boston. She became a teacher and began writing about the difficulties experienced by Native Americans. Bonnin died in 1938 and is buried in Arlington National Cemetery.

In collaboration with Matthew K. Sniffen and Charles H. Fabens, Bonnin wrote *Oklahoma's Poor Rich Indians: An Orgy of Graft and Exploitation of the Five Civilized Tribes, Legal Robbery*. Published in 1924, the book tells of the fate of Ledcie Stechi, a seven-year-old Choctaw girl who inherited twenty acres of oil-rich land from her mother. Ledcie lived with her grandmother and they were given a monthly credit of just $15 by her guardian, Jordan Whiteman, to purchase food at a local store. Eventually the money ran out and they were forced to seek help from the townspeople. What follows is a description of Ledcie's unfortunate situation:

> The little Choctaw girl, with her feeble grandmother, came to town carrying their clothes, a bundle of faded rags in a flour sack. Ledcie was dirty, filthy, and covered with vermin. She was emaciated and weighed about 47 pounds. . . . Mr. Whiteman, evidently fearing to lose his grasp on his ward, demanded the child, and Ledcie Stechi, child of much abuse, was returned to the custody of her legal guardian 24 hours after she was taken to the school where she would have had good care. The last time the aged grandmother had seen Ledcie, and only for a few minutes, was on the 12th of July.
>
> A month later, on the 14th of August, word was brought to the hills that Ledcie was dead . . . . The following day, at dawn, before the corpse had arrived, parties of grafters arrived . . . and harassed the bereaved old grandmother about the future disposal of Ledcie's valuable properties . . .*

* Gertrude Bonnin, *Oklahoma's Poor Rich Indians: An Orgy of Graft and Exploitation of the Five Civilized Tribes, Legal Robbery* (Philadelphia, Pa.: The Indian Rights Association, 1924), 24.

of the Interior often negotiated leases at far below market value. Locking Indian nations into long-term agreements that failed to take into account either inflation or growing energy costs, the U.S. government cheated the tribes out of royalties they should have received.

Black Mesa and Laguna

Following World War II, oil companies renewed their interest in the large oil and gas fields of the Four Corners area, where Colorado, Utah, New Mexico, and Arizona meet. Mining the rich oil and gas fields on the Navajo Reservation proved to be a much-needed source of revenue for the Navajo economy, bringing in millions in oil royalties each year. Uranium mining also proved profitable, earning the tribe $65,000 in 1950. By 1954, those profits had increased to $650,000.[36]

Like many Native Americans during these federal relocation policy years, most Navajos did not want to leave the reservation. But few jobs existed on the reservation. Livestock, along with tourism and the selling of rugs and jewelry, could not support everyone. The success of oil and uranium mining seemed to point the way to the future. The Navajos decided to use their natural resources to create jobs and maintain an economic viability for their tribe. Unaware of the disaster they were about to encounter, the Navajo signed a contract with Utah Mining and Manufacturing in 1962, allowing that company to strip-mine coal on land south of the San Juan River in New Mexico. Two years later, they also leased land on Black Mesa to the Peabody Coal Company.

Strip-mining is a process that does exactly what the name suggests, utilizing "huge steam-powered shovel machines called draglines, as tall as sixteen-story buildings, weighing 27 million pounds and able to move 220 cubic yards (325 tons) of 'overburden'—earth—in a single pass."[37] Strip-mining destroys everything in its path, including agricultural lands and wildlife habitats. Huge bulldozers remove layer after layer of enormous

Until the 1950s, Navajos had traditionally relied on the profits they received from raising sheep (shown here) and selling rugs and jewelry. However, an abundance of uranium, coal, and gas lay beneath reservation soil and the Navajos began tapping this source of wealth, signing contracts with both the Peabody Coal Company and United Nuclear Corporation in the 1960s. Unfortunately, both of these companies used strip-mining techniques, effectively choking off the land and poisoning the Navajos' sheep.

expanses of land, often digging down 150 feet to reach the coal beneath. When they are finished, a gaping wasteland remains. Worse, the coal must be refined, a technique requiring large amounts of water, one of the Navajos' most precious resources. And burning the coal produces massive air pollution, damaging both the Navajo tourist industry and poisoning many of their sheep. Other Native American leaders visiting the Black Mesa site saw what Peabody had done—horrifying visual evidence that led many of them to toughen their resistance against mining on their reservations.

The worst was yet to come. In July 1979, the United States'

worst accident with radioactive material came about when United Nuclear Corporation's uranium tailings dam failed at Church Rock, which lies just off the Navajo Reservation. One hundred million gallons of radioactive water flooded into the Rio Puerco, resulting in the death of 10,000 sheep.[38]

Many Navajos had long opposed the cutting into the earth to deplete its plenty. Opponents of mining charged Navajo Chairman Peter MacDonald with cozying up too much to the energy companies. But MacDonald did not act alone and the revenues provided an understandable temptation, enabling the Navajos to fund their own legal service as well as Navajo Community College.

Like Peabody, Anaconda Corporation took advantage of Native Americans. From 1952 to 1981, it ran the world's largest uranium strip mine at Laguna Pueblo in New Mexico. Like the Navajos, the Pueblos are too isolated to attract outside business interest. The mine at Laguna provided jobs for hundreds of people, until the uranium ran out and the company closed its facilities. The Laguna Pueblo was left with a gaping crater and those who had relied upon the mine for regular wages now found themselves out of work. Worse, many of those miners began to show signs of illnesses produced by exposure to radiation. Homes, even water supplies, were found to be contaminated.

What happened at Black Mesa and Laguna prompted increased organization within Indian tribes, so that they could present a united front in dealing with the energy companies. In 1975, leaders representing more than twenty tribal groups formed the Council of Energy Resource Tribes (CERT) in an effort to negotiate better deals. Some have criticized CERT as an organization that has proved itself to be of little use, seeking expertise from ex-patriot Iranians who fled to the United States following the revolution that brought the Ayatollah Khomeini to power in 1979.[39]

Equal Compensation for Natural Resources?

Certainly CERT has fought an uphill battle. Its 1982 budget of $6 million was slashed in half by the Reagan administration in 1983, resulting in massive layoffs of its staff. Previously, in 1981, the president's budget had taken away monies allocated for Indian tribes, including an 82 percent cut in economic development funds. Tribes that relied on the sale of natural resources had no choice but to continue their mining operations. At least CERT drew together the collective expertise necessary to negotiate the best possible deals with energy companies. Moreover, it provided a national forum for debates that continue to take place in every Indian nation. Mining can be a source of profit but it also takes land traditionally devoted to agricultural use. And the risks can be tremendous as the experiences at Black Mesa and Laguna Pueblo proved.

The Arab OPEC (Organization of Petroleum Exporting Companies) embargo of the 1970s increased the pressure on Indian nations to permit mining on their reservations. Americans who saw gas prices increase, seemingly overnight, from 35¢ to well over $1 per gallon, were determined to find domestic sources of fuel that would free them from dependence on foreign oil—a concern still very much in the minds of Americans today. Hosts of energy companies invaded the West once again in search of sites where they could drill. Having learned their lesson from what happened at Laguna, some Indian nations, such as the Arapaho and Shoshone of the Wind River Reservation in Wyoming, negotiated extended leases with ARCO and other energy companies, thus ensuring their people continued revenue in the event the company decided to close the mine. Others, such as the New Mexico Jicarilla Apache and the Montana Assiniboine and Sioux, elected to undertake their own drilling operations. These tribes hope to maintain greater control.

But the complicated relationship between Indian nations and the United States frequently forces energy-related problems on Native Americans. Even today, the Navajos are forced to fight the resumption of uranium mining in the same area once devastated by the radioactive spill. Yet it seems likely that the U.S. government's Nuclear Regulatory Commission may approve new uranium mining that could potentially contaminate the drinking water of fifteen thousand Navajos. A groundwater hydrologist who has worked at this site, as well as at Yucca Mountain in Nevada, condemned the government's hearing: "I've never seen such poor science, poor accountability and poor traceability."[40] For the Navajos, it seems, this fight will continue for some time.

The Navajos have a similar struggle on their hands to recover revenue lost when then-Secretary of the Interior Donald Hodel worked with Peabody Coal Company to convince the tribe to accept a lower than normal royalty payment. Despite all the damage Peabody did, they refuse to accept liability, compelling the Navajos to seek some $600 million in lost royalties from the Department of the Interior for failure to fulfill its trust obligations. In 2003, the Supreme Court rejected the case, but a federal appeals court has ruled that the Navajo suit may continue. Other Indian nations are seeking lost royalties as well. The validity of their claims is evident. For example, in 1980 when OPEC nations charged $40 per barrel of oil, the tribes received, on average, only $2 per barrel.[41]

Many Indian nations have cultural as well as environmental concerns. A proposed coal mine expansion in North Dakota, the largest in that state's history, would disturb an estimated two thousand ancient sites, including stone rings, cairns, and stone alignments scattered throughout the area.[42] But the chances of the Sioux people being able to stop this expansion are slim in the current era of court rulings that rarely side with Native Americans.

Energy Policy Act of 2003

Of greater concern was the 2003 energy bill, which was described at the last annual meeting of the National Congress of American Indians as "corporate-welfare for the rich and corporate-rape of Mother Earth." At stake is the Bush administration's attempt to recognize self-proclaimed Native Americans in Alaska as tribes in order that energy companies may secure leases for drilling. This question of the federal government declaring who is Native American smacked too much of old techniques, commonly used in the nineteenth century, of finding someone, plying him with alcohol, declaring him a chief, and then getting the necessary signature to cede lands. Almost all of the members representing tribes in the lower forty-eight states stood firm with their Alaskan allies. Gwich'in elder Jonathan Solomon charged, "We need tribes talking to tribes, not corporate money." Zuni Pueblo governor Arlen P. Quetawki supported him, saying he also had been given a sacred trust to safeguard his peoples' lands and not let anyone cut into the earth for coal, oil, or gas. "I am not about to allow anyone to come in and take them from me. . . . Pretty soon you will run out of them." For Indians, he said, our true riches lie in language, religion, and culture. "If those run out where do you expect to be!"[43]

This energy bill employs the old federal policy of offering a carrot and a stick. Hoping to win Native American support, the Republican-backed measure offers up to $22 million in loan guarantees and grants over ten years to those tribes wishing to develop their energy resources. But the bill would also reduce the Department of the Interior's trust responsibility and thus its liability for abuses that would most likely result from corporate greed. Native Americans are all too aware of the destruction those companies have wreaked on their land in the past and the reluctance of the Department of the Interior to make good on its promises. As a result, the National Council of American Indians voted overwhelmingly to urge the Senate to kill the bill.[44]

A Necessary Evil?

Other Indian nations have embraced similar sentiments when

it comes to energy development. In 1982, Congress passed the Indian Mineral Development Act to encourage Native Americans to use mining as a means of economic self-sufficiency. Under this law, Indian tribes could now become energy producers, rather than simply royalty holders at rates negotiated for them by the Department of the Interior. At the same time, Congress enacted the Indian Tribal Governmental Tax Status Act. Now tribes could issue tax-exempt revenue bonds, a necessary aid to attracting corporate investment.

Some nations, such as the Northern Cheyenne in Montana, who sit on somewhere between 20 and 50 million tons of coal, refuse to allow their land to be strip-mined. Other nations, like the Arapaho and the Shoshone, have taken advantage of federal law, which gives them greater economic control and allows them to negotiate their own leases. The days when one "good old boy" in Interior could do a favor for another "good old boy" in a corporate suit are over, though the struggle continues. The corporations are not going away; nor are the United States' energy needs. New strategies to seize Indian natural resources will be developed and Native Americans are preparing to meet them.

The reality for most Native Americans is that energy development is a necessary evil. In this growing age of energy demands, Native Americans have good reason to fear that if they do not negotiate, the U.S. government will simply find a way to take what it wants—the old threat of termination. Moreover, ongoing poverty compels the tribes that have natural resources to consider negotiated deals with the energy companies; but in recent years, the emphasis has shifted to tribal control and protection of the land. The Navajos, for example, have established their own environmental protection agency. In 1987, both the Navajos and their neighbors, the Hopis, secured new, more beneficial leases from Peabody Coal. Royalties from coal provided nearly three-quarters of the Navajo Nation's operating budget in 1996. Lacking other sources of revenue, they must deal with the energy companies.[45]

Poverty indeed remains the primary motivator when it comes to Native American communities and the energy corporations. Across the country, Americans want electricity, heating, and air-conditioning—all the comforts of modern life. At the same time, they do not want nuclear power plants, oil refineries, gas storage facilities, and, most of all, the waste by-products of those industries in their backyards. Obviously Indian nations do not want these dangers close to their children either. But in the absence of other revenues, difficult decisions have to be made.

The Passamaquoddy tribe, which has a small reservation on the coast of Maine, serves as an example of a Native American group that has been backed into a corner. Non-Indian voters throughout New England rejected their own communities as sites for the construction of tankers holding liquefied natural gas. But with an unemployment rate of approximately 50 percent, the tribe has signed a deal with Quoddy Bay LLC, a developer that has promised annual payments ranging from $4 million to $20 million in exchange for terminal development on the reservation. The dangers to the beautiful tree-lined coast are obvious, but the tribe feels they have no other option. State voters denied a recent Indian casino proposal, so the area ironically known as Pleasant Point will now become a storage facility for those tankers. As tribal representative Fred Moore III explained, "This is not about LNG (liquefied natural gas) so much as it's about the future of our tribe."[46]

Similar pressure to find revenues to maintain economic viability has led other tribes to accept monies from the U.S. Department of Energy, which has used $100,000 in study grants to explore the feasibility of storing nuclear waste in temporary facilities on tribal lands until a permanent DOE site at Yucca Mountain, Nevada, is ready. In 1994, the Mescalero

Apache Tribal Council entered into an arrangement with Minnesota's Northern States Power Company to accept 40,000 metric tons of spent nuclear fuel from these power plants. Many tribal members vehemently opposed this decision.[47]

Although questions surrounding nuclear waste receive the most attention, reservations are also approached to provide landfills for our country's other garbage—simple trash, the sort everyone throws out daily. Large urban centers, such as New York and Los Angeles, as well as other cities, generate tons of garbage daily. In the 1990s, the small Campo Reservation in San Diego County, California, began construction of a commercial facility to serve the needs of Southern California. Environmentalists immediately sprang into action, supported by non-Indian residents who feared that any resulting pollution would contaminate their drinking water as well. Yet the Campos resisted the efforts of the mostly white groups who tried to act as their defenders. The Campos found their attitude to be paternalistic—the Great White Father once again deciding what was best for Native Americans. Determined to build a commercial landfill, the Campos proclaimed that they were intelligent enough to protect themselves and the environment.[48]

Environmentalists have long charged that using reservations to dump America's garbage is naked racism. Everyone deplores corporate and government exploitation of Native American poverty. Yet the issues are not simple. Environmentalists are well-meaning but the fact remains: If Native Americans want to keep their reservation homelands intact, they often must make difficult decisions to find the revenues and develop jobs to support their people.

In an interesting example of turning the tables, one Indian nation, the Delaware of Anadarko, Oklahoma, have been trying to buy 480 acres of land in Maryland—some 1,400 miles from their reservation—to operate a landfill. The company, National Waste Managers, is anxious to work with the Delaware Indians and the tribe could certainly use the revenues, but community and state opposition has delayed the project for more than fifteen years.[49]

Throughout the country, the debate continues on many reservations. Native Americans do not want their lands to be used as waste dumps; nor do they want the pollution that, in the absence of adequate government regulation, seems to go hand-in-hand with mining operations. But to maintain cultural integrity, tribal communities must be kept intact and that requires economic viability. In the absence of other business enterprises, many Indian nations will have to continue to rely upon their energy resources and even make the wrenching decision to use part of their land as a dumping ground for off-reservation industries.

5

Business Development

THE U.S. GOVERNMENT'S RELATIONSHIP WITH NATIVE AMERICANS

As discussed in chapter 2, U.S. government efforts to end Termination and devote new attention to Native American issues, particularly poverty, in the 1960s and 1970s not only resulted in important legislation, but also in the creation of new agencies, most importantly the Office of Economic Opportunity (OEO), which worked in conjunction with the Bureau of Indian Affairs (BIA) and the Indian Financing Act of 1974 to promote reservation businesses. Specifically, the Indian Financing Act created a fund to supply grants to tribal businesses, which was absolutely necessary during an era in which most financial institutions were markedly wary of lending money to Indians. On behalf of their shareholders, banks refused to take the risk. The Indian Financing Act provided the requisite seed money to get Indian owned and operated businesses up and running.

Reclamation Projects

Legislation served as a small attempt to redress the steps the federal government had taken in the past to destroy the livelihoods of Native Americans. Perhaps the most prominent example was the Sheep Reduction Program carried out by federal agents, which began in 1936, despite Navajo objections. Soil erosion and the ongoing drought of the 1920s had led the U.S. government to conclude the open range of the reservation was being destroyed by the presence of too many grazing animals. The Navajo Tribal Council tried to cooperate with federal mandates, agreeing that all Navajos would accept a 10 percent reduction of their herds. At the same time, they urged Commissioner of Indian Affairs John Collier to provide funds available under the Indian Reorganization Act to add more grazing land to the reservation. Like many Native Americans, the Navajos value their horses. Equally important are sheep—a source of wool for the rug weaving encouraged by area traders and a food source.

Well-intentioned, but often blind to any viewpoint other than his own, Collier ordered his agents to begin slaughtering livestock. Horses and sheep were driven away while their owners were forcibly restrained (some were even jailed). The animals were shot and left to rot where they fell. Today bitter memories of those years of livestock reduction remain strong among the Navajos, who saw those horrors carried out as yet another example of federal government paternalism (Great White Father knows best) and an attack on both traditional culture and those families' livelihoods.[50]

In other parts of the country, federal reclamation projects destroyed Native American lands previously used for grazing. Growing populations on the Great Plains demanded water and electrical power. To meet these needs, the Army Corps of Engineers and the Bureau of Reclamation worked together to build dams, often flooding Indian land. One outrageous example was the Pick-Sloan Project in the Missouri River Basin. First planned in 1944, three dams were eventually built, flooding more than 202,000 acres of Sioux land on the Cheyenne River, Crow Creek, Lower Brulé, Standing Rock, and Yankton reservations in North and South Dakota.

In the East, the most famous example of federal relocation policies that destroyed Indian land came in 1964, when the Army Corps of Engineers built Kinzua Dam on the Seneca Allegany Reservation in New York. The resulting Kinzua Reservoir flooded 10,000 acres—nearly one-third of the reservation—in defiance of a 1794 treaty guaranteeing the protection of Seneca lands. More than six hundred families were forcibly removed before their homes were destroyed.[51]

Relocation Work

Having been urged by missionaries and federal agents to pursue limited education to develop skills that suited them only for home industries, agriculture, or menial jobs, few Native Americans possessed any real business knowledge in the 1960s and 1970s. Outside corporate interests that could be persuaded to open plants on reservation land generally did so to take advantage of federal incentive grants, as well as low labor costs. One BIA study revealed that "of 48 families employed during 1960–1965 by a manufacturing firm operating on the Pine Ridge Reservation of South Dakota, 31 remained below a $3,000 poverty level of income."[52]

Other tribes that had been successful in relying upon their natural resources to build prosperous industries, such as the Menominees of Wisconsin with their lumber mills, saw their businesses destroyed and their land seized under Termination policies in the 1960s.[53] Forced to leave their homes to seek jobs in nearby communities like Milwaukee, large numbers of Menominees joined the ranks of the Indian urban poor.

The U.S. government had promised jobs to those uprooted by Termination—good ones according to the pamphlets circulated in Indian country. Instead, relocation workers referred Native Americans to business owners who had agreed to hire

Following World War II, many Native Americans were uprooted from their reservation homes by the federal government with the promise of jobs in industrial centers such as Chicago, Denver, and New York. Many Iroquois men—such as these Mohawks—took jobs as "beam-walkers"; working on high-steel construction sites in cities like New York.

them, almost always low-paying factory work that proved to be temporary.[54]

Many other Native Americans had no option but to seek jobs off the reservation. Among the best known, certainly the most visible, are the "beam-walkers"—those Iroquois men who work on high-rise construction sites in Rochester and Syracuse,

New York, as well as other cities. These steelworkers find jobs close to home when they can (Onondaga men are usually the ones seen scaling the heights in Rochester and Syracuse), but they are a common-enough sight in Manhattan, too.

Other Native Americans tried to operate their own small businesses. Visitors to the state of New York have probably seen the "smoke shops" and gas stations run by Seneca and other Iroquois peoples. Taking advantage of the guarantees provided them by the U.S. Constitution, as well as treaties with both the federal government and the state, these Indian nations are not obligated to pay state taxes and are therefore able to sell their products at far cheaper rates, an advantage that brings many non-Indians onto the reservation to buy gasoline and tobacco. These businesses achieved some success in areas like New York, where the reservations are surrounded by large non-Indian populations.

Diversifying Tribal Economies

On the larger and more isolated western reservations, business development, outside of mining and other energy industries, has proven far more difficult to achieve. A good case study can be found in an examination of the Arapahos, who share the Wind River Reservation in central Wyoming with the Shoshone Nation. Tribal income for both nations is chiefly derived from those leases the Arapaho and Shoshone were able to negotiate with the energy companies to mine petroleum deposits in the 1970s. Like other Indian nations, the Arapahos no longer rely upon the BIA to manage those royalties. Instead they sought investment expertise and formed the Northern Arapaho Business Council. (The Shoshone have a similar council.) The lion's share of those royalties is distributed to individual tribal members as a monthly per-capita payment that keeps a minimal amount of income flowing to families.

Increased U.S. government interest in the 1960s and 1970s resulted in federal officials bringing pressure to bear on the

Seneca and other New York Iroquois people often run smoke shops like this one on the Cattaraugus Seneca Reservation in western New York. Thanks to treaties with the U.S. government that protect their sovereignty, the Senecas are not obligated to pay state taxes on cigarettes and gasoline and thus can sell these products for less than their off-reservation counterparts.

Arapahos to diversify their economy. One suggestion was to use tribal funds to build a potato-processing plant in 1969. The joint council of the Arapahos and Shoshones rejected the proposal, largely in reaction to being hurt by U.S. government ideas and promises for so many decades. Or as one member of the council put it, "On this potato factory, if they want Indians to put money in it, there must be something wrong with it."[55] The business council later used funds to create an industrial park, but attracting industry to this isolated part of the West has proven problematic. Without ready consumers at hand and transportation costs made ever more prohibitive by rising gas prices, factories have good fiscal reasons not to build on the reservation.

Non-Indian businesses have attempted to use Native Americans to grab profits from federal funds set aside for Indian business development. In return for Arapaho and Shoshone cooperation, which is necessary to acquire Economic Development Administration grants, Datel Company promised three hundred jobs for Wind River people.[56] But after receiving its federal money, Datel only hired nine Native Americans and laid them off a short time later. In the years that followed, they hired a few Native Americans, but the number never exceeded twenty—nowhere near the three hundred promised jobs.[57]

Treatment like this has become commonplace in Indian country, only adding to the suspicion most people harbor regarding U.S. government programs and the corporate world. The Arapahos are well aware that their location makes outside business investment unlikely and they also fear non-Indian intrusion.

So the Arapahos, like many of the energy tribes, remain reliant upon their oil and gas resources. Family income fluctuates up or down depending on energy prices at the time. This is one reason the Arapahos must be very careful about enrollment, checking each application carefully and employing those rules adopted by the tribal council to judge who qualifies.

Addressing Poverty

Like other Indian people, the Arapahos continue to follow age-old practices to deal with poverty, ensuring that all in the community will be cared for. In the event of individual or family emergencies, the community gathers, a blanket is put on the ground, and those who can, leave money on the cloth.

Another tradition practiced among many Native Americans is the "Give Away," a ceremony commonly held following a funeral. Family members lovingly lay out the deceased's possessions while the community gathers—the women of the tribe bring pies, cakes, and other foods to feed the assembled mourners. All may take something for remembrance, but those who have no special need at the time simply help themselves to an extra piece of cake, letting those who can really use a saddle, a pair of boots, or an extra shirt to get in line first. In this way, pride is maintained and thus the sharing for communal welfare practiced by Native Americans for centuries continues.

A Rocky Relationship

This traditional Native American economy has been augmented in recent years by U.S. government programs that create jobs. Native Americans hired from the reservation are increasingly filling staff positions in the Indian Health Service (IHS) and other BIA programs. In addition, state programs, such as Meals on Wheels, are being turned over to local Native Americans to operate. In Oklahoma, where there exist more opportunities for off-reservation employment, the Cherokee Nation regularly hosts job fairs to attract the attention of local businesses.[58]

The renewed federal attention to Native Americans that came about in the 1960s and 1970s, fell off sharply in the 1980s, when aid to almost all domestic programs was drastically cut, especially those programs dealing with Indian economic development. In statements reminiscent of the early years of Termination policy, Secretary of the Interior James Watt Scoffed at what he termed, "federal socialism on reservations."[59] At times, the Reagan administration's goal seemed to be to bankrupt the tribes, undermining the advances made during the 1970s. At least some of the monies for federal programs were restored in the 1990s, only to see the cuts begin again after the 2000 election, with the support of the William Rehnquist-led Supreme Court.

Most recently, the U.S. government suspended a Montana-based program that provided agricultural loans to Native Americans in twenty-eight states.[60] In February 2004, leaders of sixteen Great Plains tribes gathered in Bismarck, North Dakota, to protest President Bush's budget proposal for fiscal 2005, which would slash funding to the BIA by $52 million and, even more critically, funding for tribal colleges by $5.2 million. Tex Hall, president of the National Congress of American Indians, criticized the administration for not recognizing the priorities of the tribes.[61]

Because of their unique trustee relationship with the United States, Native Americans—these nations within a nation—are reliant upon the honorable behavior of the U.S.

An Alien Environment

In his book, *The Urban Indian Experience in America*, Donald L. Fixico opens each chapter with the story of a Sioux World War II veteran who moved to Chicago, one of the thousands relocated during the postwar years. The final excerpt of this man's story provides a good account of the realities facing many urban Native Americans in the last decades of the twentieth century:

Many things had happened since he left that one cold morning to catch the bus to Chicago to go on relocation. Now, he lived in a different reality; had even drunk for a while to escape the abrasive white man's society. As the sun rose this morning, he got up and dressed, thinking about being home again on the reservation. His parents were still there, and most of his brothers and sisters, and he missed them. His wife still lay sleeping, having worked overtime at the restaurant through the dinner shift. Reaching for the doorknob, he looked over his shoulder toward the other bedroom and living room where the children slept. His mind paused. He felt tired, but he had to go to work, to earn enough money for them. His life had been hard; living in the white man's city was harder. At times, he felt lost in the white man's world. He hoped their lives would be easier–that one day they could learn about being Lakota and Mohawk–and then he stepped into the street to catch the bus to go to work.*

* Donald L. Fixico, *The Urban Indian Experience in America* (Albuquerque, N.M.: University of New Mexico Press, 2000), 172–173.

government in keeping its treaty promises. However, Native Americans learned long ago that their survival depends on their own actions, not those made by federal officials.

Off the Reservation

While most of the federal programs designed to promote Native American economies focused on the reservation, the reality remains that more Native Americans live off the reservation than on it. What of those people who live in cities or border towns near the reservation? Lack of jobs on many reservations or the desire to seek educational opportunities have compelled many Native Americans to move away from their traditional communities throughout the twentieth century. Termination policy in the 1950s and 1960s uprooted thousands more, compelling their relocation to nearby cities. Los Angeles, Albuquerque, Minneapolis-St. Paul, San Francisco, and Chicago were among the cities receiving the largest numbers of Native American migrants.

Life was tough for those first peoples who found themselves in the alien environment of America's cities, facing new problems they had not encountered on the reservation—crime, discrimination, and racism were among the most prevalent. Many found housing in poorer areas that grew into enclaves of Native American settlement. Here, tribal lines became blurred, certainly by the third generation of urban inhabitants, and many young people began to identify themselves as Indian— not Sioux or Chippewa or any of the other tribal affiliations that had been important to their parents and grandparents.

In 1975, Congress passed H.R. 14449 to provide funding for the establishment of urban Indian centers, and within a short amount of time, fifty-eight centers had opened their doors to provide refuge, economic assistance, and simply survival advice in the cities. But such federal funding is always distributed as grants; that is, "soft money," meaning the funds may be in place one year and withdrawn the next. In 1970, the

United Indian Development Association was founded in Los Angeles to provide free technical assistance and advice to more than 450 Indian businesses in California. Within the decade, more than 1,700 jobs were created within Indian enterprises.[62]

Today, there exist hundreds of Indian-owned businesses in various cities throughout the United States. The 1990s witnessed a growing number of Indian arts and crafts shops, a sort of extension of the tourism industry. Perhaps far too many cater to the fascination with the New Age phenomena that seized popular attention in the 1990s—many selling dream catchers, beaded jewelry, and other items to people in search of spiritual growth. Some critics have charged that these businesses are cheapening Native American heritage—an issue certainly up for debate.

But the reality for most urban Native Americans is the continuing struggle to find employment and decent housing in which they can raise their children in an environment in which racism is still all too prevalent. They also worry about how much their children will understand about what it means to be Native American, as they watch them fall prey to the newest fads and other materialistic belongings acquired by their non-Indian classmates. According to the 1990 U.S. Census, 63 percent of all Native Americans lived in cities and suburbs away from the reservation. Only in 2000 did that trend begin to reverse itself, as more people returned to the reservation. The start of this demographic shift was made possible, in large part, by the expansion of the gaming industry on the reservations and the jobs those businesses created.

6

Gaming

◆ · ◆ · ◆

The focal point of much of the discussion of Indian economic development over the last two decades has centered on the issue of casino gambling. In 1979, the Seminoles in Florida opened a bingo hall, with jackpots of $10,000, in defiance of a state law prohibiting prizes exceeding $100. The success of that first small venture in bringing money, largely from non-Indian tourists, onto the reservation encouraged other Indian nations to follow suit and open gambling establishments.

CASINOS AND GAMING HALLS

Predictably, federal court cases were almost immediately filed by the states. In 1983, the U.S. 5th Circuit Court of Appeals ruled that because Florida permitted bingo halls off the reservation, it could not prohibit them on the reservation. Moreover, the U.S. Constitution specifically delegates all power to regulate commerce with the Indian nations to the federal government. Thus, the Court ruled, Florida had no power to regulate bingo among the Seminoles.[63] Four years later, the Supreme Court ruled in a California case that if the state permitted gambling in any form, it could not prohibit it on Indian reservations. Again, the Constitution's guarantees of Native American sovereignty were invoked—the state could not place controls over tribal government activities.[64]

In 1988, Congress passed the Indian Gaming Regulatory Act, which sought to limit the types of gaming Indian governments could establish without working in consultation with the states. Purely social games, or those offering only minimal prizes, remained under the sole jurisdiction of the tribe. Bingo and other such games still fell under tribal governance but also became subject to regulation by the National Indian Gaming Commission (NIGC). All other forms of gambling—slot machines, casino games, horse and dog racing, etc.—involved the National Indian Gaming Commission more heavily and required the tribes to enter into negotiations with the states in which their reservations were located.

More than any other business activity, gambling operations have brought real benefits to reservation economies. As a result, casino activity has exploded throughout Indian country over the last two decades. Some operations began and stayed relatively small, such as the Seneca Nation's Bingo Hall on the Cattaraugus Reservation in western New York. Nonetheless, busloads of off-reservation visitors travel down every week from Buffalo and other surrounding areas to play. On the other end of the scale is Foxwoods, the Mashantucket Pequot casino at Ledyard, Connecticut, which claims to be the largest casino in the world.

Foxwoods

On average, some fifty thousand people visit Foxwoods casino *daily*. In addition to its roulette tables, slot machines, and all

Over the past couple of decades, gaming has become the most profitable business venture for Native Americans. Though some tribes, such as the Hopi, oppose gaming, many tribes benefit from its profitability and use the earnings to fund education and health care. Shown here is the Seneca Nation Bingo Hall on the Cattaraugus Reservation in western New York.

the other gambling paraphernalia, the resort complex includes hotels, a sports arena, gourmet restaurants, and several theaters that feature famous entertainers and draw large numbers of visitors. By the mid-1990s, it was estimated that casino revenues alone accounted for more than $900 million annually, "more than twice the winnings of the premier Las Vegas casinos."[65]

Among both Indian and non-Indians, there exist critics who accuse the Pequot and other tribes of betraying their heritage. They have "sold out," succumbing to a greed for material acquisition, more associated with Anglo than Native American cultures. In some Indian nations, the debate continues with one group of tribal members pushing for gambling operations, while others resist, usually citing traditional laws and customs.

A Stable Source of Income

Many Indian nations believed that gaming was a logical and lucrative choice that would bring in much-needed revenue to the reservations. Farming and ranching, which were long-practiced ways of making a living, had been undercut by federal policies in the nineteenth and twentieth century. The best land was stolen and, in some cases, most notably among the Sioux of the Upper Missouri River Basin and on the Seneca Allegany Reservation, with the construction of Kinzua Dam, grazing and farmlands were flooded, as well as peoples' homes. Well-intentioned but incredibly harsh federal efforts, such as the Navajo Stock Reduction Program in the 1930s, had severely constrained tribal efforts to become self-sufficient and forced the Navajos to fall back on tourism (rug weaving and jewelry making). As discussed in chapter 3, tourism has rarely proven to be a successful source of sustainable tribal revenue. American business has also been reluctant to invest in Indian country—in many cases doing so only to take advantage of federal loan monies earmarked for Indian economic development, as was the case among the Arapaho, discussed in chapter 5. Those tribes possessing valuable energy resources have been able to negotiate leases with gas and oil companies, but fossil fuels are a finite resource. One day, they will be gone and where will those tribes find their revenues then? In any case, most reservation mining continues to rely on Anglo-dominated petroleum companies, a business reality that reduces the tribes to colonial status. They produce the raw goods, but they do not reap the ultimate profits. As discussed in chapter 4, mining also hurts the environment and the Native Americans who live on that land.

Gambling has proven to be the single most successful enterprise Indian tribes have undertaken to gain sufficient revenues and preserve the sanctity of reservation life. "In 1998, Indian gaming was a $500 million business; in 2002, 290 Indian casinos reported a combined revenue of $12.7 billion."[66] This incredible growth has led to a number of benefits. In 2000, the U.S. Census revealed that for the first time, the trend of people leaving their reservation had been reversed. With jobs now available, Native Americans could return to their homelands, to be part of their extended families and raise their children in an environment in which they can be taught what it means to be Indian—whether that is Cherokee, Dakota, Cheyenne, or any other people.

Preserving Culture through Gaming

A hefty portion of gambling revenues has been devoted to ensuring that traditional cultures are protected, not just as colorful relics from the past, but as viable societies that will continue in the future. For example, the Foxwoods Casino made possible the construction of a $193 million museum and extensive library collection, which is open to the public. This serves as a valuable repository for scholars, but it is even more important for generations of Pequot children whose school groups crowd its exhibit halls. "We want to show that Native peoples are not a static part of history, but are still evolving, vital contributors to modern society," explained David Holahan, a Pequot spokesman. "We will show that Native peoples may not be what the public often expects or envisions them to be. That's part of the learning process."[67] This museum, like others on reservations throughout the country, enables Native Americans to define themselves, to offer public images of the real Native

American in an attempt to counter decades of inaccurate portrayals by Hollywood.

Similarly, on the Qualla Boundary in North Carolina, the Eastern Band of Cherokees entered into a business arrangement with Harrah's to build a casino. Though relatively small compared to Foxwoods, the casino at Cherokee offers twenty-four-hour-a-day gaming, as well as a theater and restaurant. To a large degree, the casino has been incorporated into the already successful tourism enterprise operated by the tribal community. It is very much designed for family entertainment and includes more than three thousand video games for children to enjoy. Like the Pequots, the Cherokees have used these casino profits to expand their already impressive museum, again primarily designed for the education of the public and, most especially, children.[68]

As always, reservation location has proven to be a primary determinant of whether gaming can be used as a successful business venture. Some Indian nations have elected to enter agreements with nearby communities, which enables them to open casinos in more heavily populated urban areas. One example is the Potawatomi Bingo Casino in Milwaukee, Wisconsin, a profitable business of the Forest County Potawatomi Tribe. This 256,000-square-foot gaming complex provides the usual slot and table games, as well as a 1,600-seat bingo hall, along with the restaurants and theaters that other tribal casino operations proved to be a vital component in attracting visitors.[69]

Profits and Benefits

The Bureau of Indian Affairs (BIA) reported in 1999 that 212 tribes in 24 states operated 267 casinos. Although Indian gaming represents less than 10 percent of all gambling in the United States, the profits generated have made an enormous difference to many reservations. Over the last several decades, unemployment has grown sharply in the nation's industrial rustbelt of the Midwest, as factories closed and people lost their jobs. Jobs are particularly scarce in western New York and indeed throughout much of upstate New York. Profits gained from the operation of the Stone Casino resort in Verona enabled the Oneida Nation to offer $3.7 million in bonuses to its 3,700 full-time workers in 2003.[70] These checks were paid both to Oneida workers and non-Indian employees, too.

Similarly, the Cherokee Nation Enterprises, which operates Cherokee Casinos in Oklahoma, shares gaming revenues with non-Indians around them. In 2003, casino profits were used to charter buses to bring six hundred members of the Oklahoma Army National Guard's 120th Engineer battalion home to their families during Christmas. Fearing that many of these soldiers might be deployed abroad by the following Christmas, the Cherokees wanted to make sure they could be with their families in 2003.

Chad Smith, principal chief of the Cherokee Nation, explained: "Some of these soldiers work for the Cherokee Nation. Many more are our friends, family members and neighbors. We wanted to give them a chance to come home, because they are doing so much for us."[71]

Another example of how Indian nations share the benefits gained through gaming with their non-Native American neighbors can be found in California, where Indian tribes donate money to fund Indian studies programs at universities throughout the state. Arguing that university programs in Indian studies have long been underfunded, the San Manuel Band of Mission Indians gave $4 million to the UCLA Law School to establish a new center to develop courses on Indian issues and provide tribal internships.[72] The same tribe had almost all of its 850-acre reservation stripped bare by wildfires in 2003 and donated $1 million to the area's disaster relief fund.[73]

Improved schools, new homes for the elderly, increased health care, tribal scholarships, and jobs—these are just some of the benefits gaming has brought to Indian reservations. As previously mentioned, Native Americans share their gaming profits with the surrounding communities. Gaming has also led to instances of inter-tribal cooperation. In October 2003, the Yavapai Nation of Arizona, successful operators of the Cliff Castle Casino, north of Phoenix, signed a letter of intent with the La Posta Band of Mission Indians in California to help them secure a loan and develop a casino. The Yavapais will help hire and train staff but full management of the casino will be left in the hands of the La Posta Band.[74]

In Minnesota, the Shakopee Mdewakanton Sioux Community has used gaming to create a thriving reservation economy, and, in November 2003, agreed to loan $42 million to the Leech Lake Band of Ojibwe. This loan was one of the largest transactions ever to take place between two tribes.[75]

So have casinos effectively alleviated poverty throughout Indian country? Of course not. Not all casino businesses have been successful. Seven years ago the Kaibab Band of Paiutes' Pipe Spring Casino had to close in Arizona. It simply failed to attract enough tourists to make a profit.[76]

Native American Opposition to Casinos

Other nations reject casino operations as being contrary to traditional tribal teachings. In May 2004, the Hopis voted down a proposal that would have built a casino near Winslow, Arizona. Fearing outside influences that might damage Hopi cultural values, one opponent, Vernon Masayesva, urged his fellow Hopis to vote no as a way to honor their ancestors who had created a sanctuary for the people, where they might follow Haso'gada's way of life. "They were refugees running away to escape Koyaanisqatsi, a world turned upside down. Here on the fingerprints of Black Mesa, they found the place." Tribal vice chairman, Caleb Johnson explained Hopi opposition in terms the non-Indian world might better understand: "Gaming is making money off other people's bad habits, and the Hopi way says we should not use other people's bad habits to benefit."[77]

Over the last ten years, the Navajos have held three refer-
endums on the issue of whether to establish some form of
gaming on their vast reservation. One group of Navajos has
recently opted to begin casino operations, but it remains to be
seen if gaming will prove to be profitable. Obviously the
Navajos, like all Native Americans, need the revenue—but not
enough to overturn cultural traditions. The enormity of the
Navajo Reservation has enabled those people who wish to live
apart from non-Indian society to do so. Unlike other peoples
who have been forced to acculturate their lives to Anglo-
America, many Navajos continue to live traditional lives.
Navajo is very much a living language, commonly spoken.
Many elderly have never learned English; there was no need.
Building casinos would change that way of life.

Continued Growth of Casinos

Las Vegas-based casinos, such as Harrah's, stand ready to invest
in Indian country. Most recently, they have joined with the
Narragansett Indians of Rhode Island to petition the state for
approval to build a $450 million casino in West Warwick,
which they promise would create thousands of jobs and generate annual revenues for the state in excess of $100 million.[78]
Some tribes, like the Eastern Band of Cherokees, used Harrah's
investment to generate sufficient income so that they could
eventually build their own casino. In December 2003, construction began on a new hotel tower that promises to double
existing gambling and entertainment offerings. The difference
this time is that the Cherokees are building without outside
help. The tribe borrowed $69 million for the construction and
has assumed responsibility for the existing debt of all gambling complexes on the Qualla Boundary, at a total cost of
$175 million.[79] The willingness of banks to provide these loans
proves that the Cherokees are considered a good investment by
financial lenders, a marked change from only two decades ago.

Grabbing a Share of the Profits

The remarkable revenues casino resorts brought to hundreds of reservations was bound to attract the interest of states that were looking to obtain a share of these profits. Under the provisions of the Indian Gaming Regulatory Act (IGRA), those tribes conducting Class III gambling operations (slots, roulette, table games, etc., for major prizes) must negotiate compacts with the states in which they are located. While the IGRA requires that tribal governments must be the sole owners and primary beneficiaries of gaming and that proceeds be used to promote economic development, there is considerable latitude for state interference. IGRA regulations, such as that "the State shall negotiate with the Indian tribe in good faith", have been strained in recent years, as various states have delayed discussions in an effort to prompt Indian nations to agree to turn over larger shares of their profits.

In 2004, Minnesota governor Tim Pawlenty challenged the monopoly of the state's eighteen tribal casinos. While the governor's office will confirm no specifics about the changes he wants in the fifteen-year-old agreement between the tribes and the states, some lawmakers speculate that Pawlenty is threatening state-sanctioned competition unless the tribes renegotiate their contract to the state's advantage.[80] In Wisconsin, the Republican-controlled legislature has asked the courts to void the Indian gaming contracts signed by Democratic governor Jim Doyle.[81] The ability of the states to play hardball when it comes to trying to secure gaming revenues at the expense of their Indian citizens was perhaps most flagrantly demonstrated in Maine, where in November 2003, the state voted down a $650 million casino project proposed by the Penobscots and Passamaquoddies, as a venture to create thousands of jobs and keep their young people from leaving the state. That same day, Maine voters approved a plan to add slot machines at the state's harness racing tracks.

In an effort to offset state opposition, Indian nations from

New York to California have made generous contributions to support local school districts, build youth clubs, and fund a host of other public ventures in return for state cooperation. But Indian success in casino development pointed the way to new and speedy revenues for states anxious to augment their own dwindling treasuries during the nation's recent economic downturn. Unfortunately, many states seem determined to follow the lead of other states, organizing their own casinos and cutting out the Native American operations.

The states are not the only opponents to Native American gambling. Gambling operations in Reno, Nevada, tried to stop casino development in Sacramento, California, that would draw business away from them. Even real estate tycoon Donald Trump brought suit in federal court, charging that Indian gaming in New York threatened his Atlantic City casinos. More recently, Trump has changed sides. According to evidence presented before a House Committee on Government Reform, Trump, along with four other financiers, has spent $35 million in Connecticut alone, trying to help would-be tribes, many of which have dubious claims to Native American identity, to win the federal recognition necessary to enable them to build casinos. If successful, those businessmen bankrolling the effort will be there to grab a sizeable share of the profits.[82]

Other Opposition to Gaming

Some states have legitimate reasons to oppose Indian gaming. Like some Native Americans, there are communities that simply do not want gambling in their midst. One example is Louisiana, where the state government refuses to consider the Jena Band of Choctaw proposal to build a casino in Logansport. The citizens of that part of the state do not want gambling.[83]

Others are concerned about the large number of wannabes who have come forward declaring themselves to be Indian, usually descendants of some historic tribe whose people died off in the first wave of disease following European contact. With the backing of non-Indian money, these people seek federal recognition necessary for them to build casinos. Rumors of organized crime involvement are commonly bantered about in these cases. What is more easily proved is that these efforts have made the long-standing work of many tribes, recognized by their states, but not the federal government, more difficult.

Federally recognized tribes are those that have a demonstrable and long-standing relationship with the United States, usually through a treaty or some other document. Termination ended federal recognition for sixty-one tribes. Five hundred and fifty-six nations remain who qualify for the protection offered by their unique trust relationship with the United States.

There exist other tribes that are recognized by their states but not by the federal government, thus rendering them ineligible for BIA aid to education and health care, as well as denying them constitutional protections against state intrusions into their affairs. Some states support their Native Americans' efforts to secure federal recognition. Virginia, for example, has eight state-recognized Indian tribes, all of which have incorporated in an effort to seek federal status. Congressman Jim Moran of Virginia and others have supported them, repeatedly introducing legislation that calls for BIA recognition and emphasizes that all of the tribes have agreed to never pursue casino gambling. In other words, they seek recognition because they are Indian, not simply because they are looking to make money.

Indian nations have taken an active role in opposing claims of some people to be Indian. The Lumbee tribe in North Carolina has sought federal recognition for more than a decade to no avail, opposed in part by the Cherokees, who insist there was no historical Lumbee tribe, no language, or common cultural heritage. Similarly, the Tulalip tribes in Washington oppose the claims of the Snohomish for federal recognition.[84]

Conclusion

The debate over casino gambling on the reservations will continue in the years ahead. Many tribes are sharply divided over the issue: some insisting that gambling violates traditional culture; others arguing that the economic well-being casino resorts provide is the only way to ensure cultural survival.

Casino gambling has brought considerable benefits to reservations and nearby communities, alike. A quarter of a million jobs have been created. In eastern states, that has enabled tribal governments to provide jobs to all of their people, as well as to many non-Indians, an important incentive in rust belt areas like western New York. The resulting tribal income has been used to improve services, promote further economic and community development, and build heritage centers like those at Foxwoods and on the Qualla Boundary. Only about one-fourth of the tribes distribute per-capita payments directly to tribal members.

In some ways, all Native Americans have benefited from the increased political clout gaming revenues have provided. Tribal governments now have money to hire the political expertise necessary to defend their rights and resources, as well as regain lands that were taken earlier. They can also afford lobbyists and seek to broaden their influence in state, as well as national elections. While President Bush has never spoken before the National Congress of American Indians, the contenders for the Democratic Party's nomination were certainly in attendance at the annual meeting in November 2003, including Wesley Clark, Dennis Kucinich, Joe Lieberman, Dick Gephardt, Howard Dean, and John Kerry, who conducted a question-and-answer session via satellite.

Gaming revenues may have brought Indian nations to the attention of federal politicians, but they have also drawn new battle lines between the tribes and those states in which they are located. NIGC regulations have compelled Indian nations to enter compacts with the states and as a result, tribal governments

Wesley Clark, a candidate for the Democratic Party presidential nomination in 2004, was one of several Democrats who spoke in front of the National Congress of American Indians' annual meeting in November 2003. The revenue generated from gaming has given Native Americans more political clout; they can now afford to pay lobbyists who can promote their rights. Clark is shown here with Harold Lockwood, a Vietnam veteran and member of the Laguna Pueblo.

have grown frustrated at the delays that state governors and/or legislatures employ in an effort to secure a larger share of the profits for themselves. The states have played one tribe against another in some cases. Elsewhere, the states have offered tax incentives to entrepreneurs to build casinos that challenge reservation businesses. But Indian gaming is here to stay. Are the Indian nations truly sovereign? That seems to be the issue at the forefront of a growing confrontation between Native Americans and the states.

7

Sovereignty versus the State

-◇-·-◇-·-◇-

PROTECTING NATIVE AMERICAN RIGHTS

When many people think of Indian history, they recall an adversarial stance between various tribes and the U.S. government—a sort of redskins versus the cavalry movie image. In reality, the chief adversary, especially when it comes to economic issues, has been the state. This was true in the 1830s after gold was discovered on Cherokee land at Dahlonega. Georgia wanted to push the Cherokees out and take the gold, as well as the valuable farming land, for themselves. To accomplish that removal, Georgians and many other westerners elected well-known Indian fighter Andrew Jackson to the presidency. But while Jackson certainly supported Georgia, it was another branch of the federal government, the Supreme Court, which defended Native Americans. Indeed, the famous ruling written by Chief Justice John Marshall, which defined Indians as "domestic, dependent nations", in *Cherokee Nation v. Georgia*, stands as one of the pillars of law today in underscoring the sovereignty of Native Americans.

Over the last few decades, the courts have proven to be far less of a friend to Native Americans. State ambitions for Indian land and resources has never slackened. For example, Native Americans earning money within Indian country are not subject to state taxes—either income or sales taxes. In 2003 when New Mexico collected state income taxes on military salaries due to Pueblo veterans living on the reservations, the federal court refused to hear the case.[85]

Native Americans have long had to contend with the states to protect their rights to natural resources. In the West, this primarily means water. The 1908 Winters Doctrine upheld Blackfeet rights, but it remained primarily a paper victory for decades. Today the fight for water continues. For example in 2004, environmentalists joined forces with the Hoopa Valley Tribe to counter California efforts to block restoration of the Trinity River, arguing, "For at least 10,000 years, Native Americans along the rivers have depended on healthy rivers and sustainable salmon populations as part of their culture and economy."[86]

Most Indian nations today make every effort to reach compromise solutions that will satisfy the economic needs of both the reservations and the states. Yet the issue of taxation remains. Two case studies—New York and California—will be used here as examples of continuing state inroads on Indian sovereignty.

Pataki's War

In upstate New York, many Indian reservations developed small business operations; selling gasoline and cigarettes at far cheaper prices because they were not obligated to add state sales tax. Most of these stores are small buildings, generally called smoke shops because of the availability of cheap tobacco there. In addition, some stores offered handcrafts and jewelry

New York's proposed taxation of cigarettes and gasoline sold by the Seneca Nation on reservation lands has been a point of contention between the Senecas and Governor George Pataki in recent years. Though the State of New York could use the funds generated from the tax, the Senecas are steadfast in protecting their sovereignty, which is supported by both the U.S. Constitution and treaties with the federal government. Shown here are Seneca protestors on the Cattaraugus Reservation, south of Buffalo, New York.

designed for a non-Indian tourist market—dream catchers, Indian dolls, beaded necklaces, and so on. Like many states caught up in the declining industrial economy at the end of the twentieth century, New York suffers large unemployment rates. After he was elected in 1992, Governor George Pataki seemed determined to find additional state revenues by collecting state sales taxes on the reservation, in defiance both of Constitutional guarantees to Native Americans, which defined them as sovereign nations, and of state treaties.

Some of the Iroquois governments bowed to the intense pressure Pataki brought to bear, seeking negotiated settlements with the state. One nation, the Seneca, held out, citing the

Buffalo Creek Treaty of 1842, under which the state of New York had promised not to apply any taxes on Seneca land. For the Senecas, their legal rights guaranteed by both the State of New York and the U.S. Constitution seemed clear. Governor Pataki, however, had other ideas.

A series of crises followed with Indian protests closing the Thruway, the major interstate terminal that runs from west to east through New York. The situation came to a head in 1997, when Pataki ordered state troopers to surround the Seneca people on the Cattaraugus Reservation, which lies on Lake Erie, between Buffalo and Dunkirk. By the time people awoke that April morning, state police had closed every road, permitting no one to leave the reservation. Worse, nothing was permitted to be brought in—no fuel, no groceries, nothing. This author was among those who were trapped on the reservation during the days that followed.

The state police were indeed thorough, blocking not only the main road in and out of the reservation but every back trail. Standing shoulder to shoulder with their face helmets in place and billy clubs at the ready, the officers were indeed a formidable sight. And unfortunately those clubs were used in a series of skirmishes, primarily instigated by Seneca teenagers outraged at this flagrant abuse of state power. Many children were hurt, some badly enough to be taken to the hospital. But most of the officers did their best to contain the situation. They did not want to be there either, calling the situation the governor had provoked, "Pataki's War."

There were no grocery stores on the reservation; nor did most people have sufficient fuel supplies to heat their homes for long. Spring comes late in that part of New York and there was still snow on the ground. But everyone shared what they had and the Senecas held firm, refusing to cave in to the state. Eventually, public pressure forced Pataki to withdraw the state troopers; the tactic obviously was not going to work.

When we could again leave the reservation, we saw that the

local residents had tried to help. Some of them had put together homemade signs, generally pieces of plywood propped up in their yards with the words, "Leave our Indians alone" painted in bold black letters. Cynics may charge that those people only wanted to hold onto their access to cheap gas and cigarettes. In addition, there exists a good deal of regional resentment against the state capital in Albany trying to impose its will on western New York, some four hundred miles away. But there also seemed to be genuine outrage at this flagrant abuse of state power.

In any case, the Senecas on the Cattaraugus Reservation may have won that battle in 1997, but the war continues. The governor insists that the state has the right to collect sales taxes on all purchases made by non-Indians on the reservation, a stance that fails to take into account the money spent by Senecas off the reservation for just about all retail needs, from food to clothing to automobiles.

Like other Native Americans nationwide, the Senecas have grown sophisticated in their knowledge about how to fight back. Drawing upon the lessons learned during the "fish-ins" in Washington State and other resistance activities of the 1970s, the Senecas turned to the media to make their case. At present, an "Honor Indian Treaties" series of television advertisements continues to raise public awareness in New York, as is evidenced by the growing numbers of letters state lawmakers say they are receiving from their constituents.[87]

Unable to collect taxes from Seneca retailers, the state has gone after their wholesale suppliers. The New York Department of Taxation and Finance has announced its intention to collect the $1.50 per pack state tax on cigarettes from companies before they will be allowed to deliver to reservation stores.

Encouraged by the Seneca example, the Cayugas recently started their own petition drive to counter New York's efforts to tax wholesalers. Other Indian nations in western New York are following suit.[88]

In an effort to try and circumvent the governor's plans, the Senecas began using the Internet to sell tobacco in direct defiance of a state law banning such sales. In this case, legal precedent has been established: The law against Internet sales of tobacco was passed in 2000, both for the sake of public health and to prevent the sale of cigarettes to minors. The latter is a hard argument to counter. Thankfully, current statistics show that increasing numbers of young people today refuse to fall prey to nicotine addiction. An additional reality is that few teenagers use the Internet to buy cigarettes, which would then be delivered to their homes and raise questions from their parents. It is far easier to find a friend with a real or fake ID to buy a pack locally. So despite its noble window-dressing, the state's real goal continues to be to collect sales taxes on reservation transactions.

The Seneca Nation licenses all tobacco merchants on Seneca land (the Senecas are divided primarily onto two reservations—the Cattaraugus and the Allegany). Proceeds from those licensing fees are used to support the nation's services to its people. The online cigarette trade alone provides jobs to 1,500 people, vital employment in a region where factory closures and a depressed economy mean there are simply no other jobs available. The local U.S. district court rejected a previous case brought by the Senecas to challenge the Internet ban. In January 2004, the Senecas filed a new suit, though few believe it will be successful.[89] In reality, the Senecas are fighting a losing battle against the state. And, in the end, it seems that the Senecas, like so many others, will have to turn to casino gambling to find the revenues to keep their nation intact (The Seneca Allegany Casino recently opened in Salamanca, New York.) While there have been bingo halls on both the Cattaraugus and Allegany reservations for many years, many Senecas actively oppose them, and it seems that this issue will now divide the Senecas as well.

Governor Pataki supports this economic endeavor,

encouraging casino construction in nearby Buffalo to be operated by the Seneca Nation. Under the compact provisions of the
Indian Gaming Regulatory Act, New York will be assured of
sizeable proceeds from Seneca casinos. But the cat and mouse
game between New York and its Native Americans continues
with the state's general assembly first voting to provide the
Senecas with land in downtown Buffalo and then delaying
negotiations over construction, most likely with an eye to secur-
ing the best possible deal for the state. Meanwhile, the governor
continues to try to collect state taxes on tobacco sales, most
recently targeting the two Indian reservations—Poosepatuck
and Shinnecock—on Long Island.[90]

The Senecas' fight over the state's intention to collect sales

The President of the Seneca Nation Speaks on Tribal Sovereignty

The ongoing dispute over taxation between the Seneca Nation and the State
of New York has been a point of contention for years: The Senecas have spent
millions of dollars in advertising in defending their sovereignty; using the
slogan—Break a Treaty, Break the Law. Conversely, the State of New York
relies upon the $1.50-a-pack tax on cigarettes and the 28.95-cent-a-gallon tax
on gasoline to generate state revenues and had planned to include the $186
million in revenues it would receive from the taxes on goods sold on Seneca
lands in its 2004 budget. However, after much public opposition, New York
first put off the taxation plan until 2005 and recently postponed it indefinitely.

Some nations, such as the St. Regis Mohawks and the Oneidas, have
agreed to the state tax in return for the construction of casinos. The Senecas,
however, have been steadfast in their opposition to Governor George Pataki's
tax plan . . . and they have the Constitution on their side: the Seneca Nation
signed federal treaties with the United States in 1794 and 1842 that protect the
sovereignty of their lands. What follows is an explanation from Seneca Nation
President Rickey L. Armstrong as to why New York's plan to tax the Senecas
is unfair:

taxes on tobacco and gasoline sold in the smoke shops provides only one case study. Similar conflicts are occurring nationwide. In July 2003, Rhode Island police engaged in a violent confrontation with the Narragansett owners of a smoke shop, closing the store and arresting seven tribal members. The Narragansetts are a federally recognized tribe; their Constitutional rights are clearly defined. Nonetheless, U.S. District Judge William Smith has upheld the state's right to tax Indian land.[91]

In other states, Native Americans have tried to reach some compromise before state troopers are sent in. The Coeur d'Alenes are among Idaho's four major Indian tribes who announced in December 2003 that they were voluntarily adding tax stamps to all cigarettes sold on the reservations.

The state Legislature adopted a provision for the 2003–2004 budget that calls for the state Department of Taxation and Finance to collect tax on the sale of tobacco and gasoline to non-Indians on Indian territories. This plan is wrong on several levels. Most importantly, the plan would violate Indian treaties. Article VI, clause 2 of the U.S. Constitution, says treaties are the "Supreme Law of the Land; and the Judges in every State should be bound thereby." The Constitution is clear; no other law can supersede a treaty. One of the best examples of a treaty that recognizes Indian tax immunity is the Buffalo Creek Compromise Treaty of 1842. This is a treaty between the Seneca Nation, the United States and the state of New York. Article 9 of the Treaty of 1842 says that Seneca Nation lands will be free "from all taxes, and assessments for roads, highways, or any other purpose until such lands shall be sold or conveyed by the said Indians."*

* Rickey L. Armstrong, Sr., President, Seneca Nation of Indians, quoted in "State Plan to Tax Gas, Tobacco Would Hurt Indian Territories," *Albany (NY) Times Union* (November 11, 2003).

California's Fiscal Crisis

California provides another case study of Native Americans trying to find the economic prosperity necessary to ensure true self-determination. In 1953, Congress passed Public Law 280, giving California and four other states jurisdiction over offenses committed on Native American lands.[92] Under this legislation, the states also assumed responsibility for some aspects of civil jurisdiction in disputes over Indian lands. They were not given the power to tax, but the law opened a new door for California to try and interfere with the economic operations of state tribes.

In the five years since California voters approved Indian gambling, Native American enterprises have exploded into a $5 billion industry, a figure that is not equally distributed among the state's Indian tribes. Of California's 107 federally recognized tribes, only 15 operate casinos with the maximum 2,000 slot machines allowed under state compact. An additional 36 tribes operate much smaller businesses of approximately 300 slot machines.[93] Thus while gambling has brought prosperity to some California Native Americans, most do not share in the wealth and remain below the poverty level.

This sudden prosperity attracted the interest of officials who were dealing with severe economic woes. In the 1990s, Governor Pete Wilson was put on the offensive when he tried to solve the state's budget shortfalls by obtaining revenue from Native American gaming. Wilson's successor, Gray Davis, was also struggling with California's fiscal crisis, when widespread alarm over the state's economy provoked the recall that removed him from office. In his place, voters sent Arnold Schwarzenegger to Sacramento.

In seeking the governorship, Schwarzenegger made taking monies away from the Indian tribes one of his campaign promises, a rather brazen public statement. Native Americans have learned from experience to view the state as their adversary,

California has long tried to solve the state's budget shortfalls by obtaining revenue from Native American gaming operations. In 2004, Governor Arnold Schwarzenegger signed a compact (shown here) with five Indian tribes that requires them to pay 8.8 percent of their revenues to the state.

but few candidates for public office risk alienating Native American voters.

But Schwarzenegger promised to go on the attack and he did. Under the compact negotiated with California, as required by the Indian Gaming Regulatory Act, the casino tribes paid 8.8

percent of their revenues to the state. Schwarzenegger pointed to two Connecticut tribes that paid 25 percent of their revenues and demanded that California tribes do the same.[94] One of his first acts upon taking office was to appoint Bay Area attorney and former appellate judge Daniel Kolkey (who had also led Indian negotiations under Pete Wilson) to deal with the tribes. Some tribes immediately expressed their willingness to increase their contributions. Speaking on those tribes' behalf, attorney Howard L. Dickstein said, "The people of California stood with the tribes when we needed them and now we want to be there for the people during the current budget crisis."[95]

Dickstein's statement put a savvy spin on what was a political reality—the casino tribes acted rapidly to maintain public goodwill in the midst of the uproar over California's fiscal difficulties. But other tribes meeting at the ninth annual Western Indian Gaming Conference at the Palm Springs Convention Center that January expressed their alarm at the precedent being set. The governor's insistence of renegotiating existing compacts flies in the face of Indian sovereignty. Moreover, the California reservation casino industry already employs more than forty-one thousand people, many of them non-Indian, and thus was already making a contribution to the state's economy.[96] In addition, many of the casino nations regularly donate hefty philanthropic contributions, totaling millions of dollars, to the state's fire-fighting efforts and public education.

What Native Americans find most insulting is the governor's refusal to wait for negotiations or to accept the word of tribal leaders that they intend to cooperate. Instead, the state administration has introduced the Gambling Revenue Act of 2004, or Proposition 68, which was scheduled for the November 2004 ballot. Fortunately for Native Americans, the proposition was overwhelmingly shot down—83.8 percent of Californians voted against it. If the legislation had been passed, then a mandatory 25 percent share of all slot machine revenues would have been collected by the state. The legislation would have presented a severe challenge to federal authority under the Indian Gaming Revenue Act of 1988.

Meanwhile, Governor Schwarzenegger has shown he intends to play hardball. In May 2004, state and federal agents raided the Coyote Valley Shodakai Casino in Redwood Valley, as well as the homes of tribal leaders, taking computers and documents in what was purported to be a search for evidence of embezzlement. Declaring that they were also looking for misuse of tribal funds, the agents took everything in what was a clear act of intimidation.[97]

Conclusion

Native Americans want to live in cooperation and goodwill with their non-Indian neighbors. Many nations initiate negotiations and participate in good faith to avoid confrontation. The Navajos negotiated with nearby communities to share limited water resources that would benefit both their agricultural co-op and the needs of nearby communities. Other examples of Indian tribes sharing with their non-Indian neighbors can be found in chapter 6.

In the view of Native Americans, their current struggles in New York, California, and elsewhere are simply a continuation of an old story. If Indians find gold, the state will try to find a way to take it. When the Cherokees discovered gold at Dahlonega in the 1830s, Georgia moved in to steal the land. When "liquid gold," that is, gas and oil were found beneath the earth of Indian Territory, the state of Oklahoma broke every moral law to strip the Indian owners of their land holdings and, in some cases, their lives. Federal funds made available through the extensive legislation of the 1960s and 1970s, which was designed to promote Indian economic development, brought corporate interests into Indian country to reap the benefits, opening plants but not employing Native Americans to work in them, as happened on the Wind River Reservation. Even worse are some of the scars left by strip-mining activities, as energy companies have destroyed the land.

Gaming and smoke-shop profits are just another piece of the story. This new Indian gold has given states a new reason to challenge Indian sovereignty. What has changed is the ability of Indian to resist—through lobbying, raising public awareness, supporting political campaigns, and in the courts—and seek legal remedies they can now afford to pursue.

But the odds remain tough in an era of marked American conservatism. Native American recognition of the battle that lies ahead was expressed in a recent editorial in *Indian Country Today*:

> The national Republican Party may be a house divided when it comes to raising or lowering taxes, but the GOP has generally closed ranks in support of taxing Indians. That is the message emanating from an emergent statehouse rebellion against the GOP line on taxation, coupled with continuing efforts by party notables to enrich state treasuries by taxing Indian gaming and cigarette sales. . . . The National Congress of American Indians, the National Indian Gaming Association, and United South and Eastern Tribes have all spoken out against the tax.[98]

Indian sovereignty is at stake. Some people contend that it no longer exists; not in the modern era. Native Americans disagree and grow angry at state attempts to override the federal trustee relationship guaranteed to Indian nations by more than four hundred treaties and, indeed, the Constitution. Anishinaabe activist Marge Anderson sums up the Indian viewpoint most succinctly:

> When Indian incomes are level with yours, when our schools are as good as yours, our houses as warm, our kids as safe and our woods and streams as clean as yours, when our babies first open their eyes to a future as bright as yours, then

we'll talk about level playing fields. Whether out of greed or out of racism or out of ignorance, there are always some who will go after Indian self-determination and economic development in ways as old as Columbus, as bold as Custer and as devious as any federal land grabber.[99]

8

Owenvsv

- ◇ - ◇ - ◇ -

We can only be what we give ourselves the power to be.
—Cherokee Feast of Days

CHALLENGES TO TODAY'S NATIVE AMERICANS

Owenvsv [pronounced Oo-way-nuh-suh] means home in the Tsalagi (Cherokee) language. Indian efforts to achieve economic self-sufficiency in the twentieth century have been undertaken to protect the homeland. The reservations are more than just places for Native Americans to live. They are cultural centers—havens where the next generation can be taught what it means to be Indian. The protection of the reservation is as important to those Native Americans who live in America's cities and suburbs as it is to the people who live within the confines of the reservation. As one worried Indian mother living in San Francisco said about her son: "He's too young to understand all that's happening around him. When he gets in high school, I'll send him back to the reservation because that's the only place he'll learn anything about life and how it is. I don't think he'll learn it here—not in the city."[100]

Returning to the Reservation

The 2000 U.S. Census showed that Native Americans were returning to reservations. Jobs created by gaming, mining, tourism, and other reservation business make it possible for people to earn a living now. More importantly, those salaries mean they can raise their children among their extended families and, as the woman quoted above says, "learn about life"— at least those lessons Native Americans value.

Five hundred years of struggling to resist conquest has taken its toll. U.S. Americanization policy, which was aimed at destroying Indian cultures through a vacillating series of government strategies—from George Washington's Gradualism through Andrew Jackson's Removal to the Allotments of the nineteenth and early twentieth centuries and Termination in the post-World War II era—brought the full power of the federal government to bear against Native Americans. Most of the land was lost; many people were stripped of their tribal identities as well. After a couple of generations away from the reservation, many Native Americans no longer see a place for themselves among the tribes of their grandparents or great-grandparents.

Bureaucracy

The real challenge to Indian nations as they move forward into the twenty-first century is federal bureaucracy. The U.S. Constitution, as well as hundreds of treaties, promises the U.S. government will acknowledge the sovereignty of Indian nations and uphold its trustee obligations. But the lessons of the past have shown that Native Americans cannot depend on any consistency in federal policy. Shifting political climates can alter policy. Programs that are in place for Indian economic

Dave Anderson, a member of the Lac Courte Oreilles band of Ojibwe, was appointed head of the Bureau of Indian Affairs by President George W. Bush in September 2003. The BIA has long been perceived by Native Americans as an ineffectual and mismanaged organization and Anderson's sudden resignation in February 2005 did nothing to help the BIA's reputation.

development one year may be withdrawn in the next administration.

The U.S. government's recognition of the importance of Native American economic development is evidenced by the September 2003 appointment of Dave Anderson to head the Bureau of Indian Affairs. An enrolled member of the Lac Courte Oreilles band of Ojibwe in Wisconsin, Anderson is a talented businessman who began with a barbeque stand and turned it into a chain of eighty-seven restaurants in twenty-three states. He holds a graduate degree in public administration from Harvard University and led Lac Courte Oreilles tribal business enterprises in the 1980s.

Unfortunately, Anderson, who stated that he felt he could do more to help Native Americans by working in the private sector, decided to resign in February 2005—only a little more than a year after he took office. Anderson's resignation only adds to the negative perception of the BIA by Native Americans—its mismanagement of Indian affairs is well documented and the problems currently facing the agency are mammoth in scope.

Because of their unique status as nations within a nation, Native Americans must work within the BIA and other government bureaucracy. At the same time, they have always known they must first and foremost look to themselves for their own survival. And they are determined survivors. That Native Americans are still here, five hundred years after the invasion began, proves that.

In the end, this is a story of success, not defeat. Despite overwhelming odds, Indian nations continue to exist. Moreover, they push forward to continue to develop economic strategies that will make certain future generations can live as tribal members.

Preserving Education

Revenues secured through gaming have been chiefly responsible for aiding the nations in the development of educational programs, which prepare their young people for the future. With economic prosperity comes political clout—enabling the nations to push for the inclusion of Native American cultures and history in public education. Some states with large Indian populations, such as Wisconsin and South Dakota, have already passed legislation mandating that Native language and history be included as part of the state curriculum. Preserving the language remains a principal concern. Arapaho and Shoshone instruction has long been available at Wyoming Indian High School on the Wind River Reservation in Wyoming. Wind River Tribal College in Ethete also teaches Arapaho and urges its students to speak the language at home as much as possible, adopting the old adage: Use it or lose it. Other nations are following suit, often hiring elders to teach the next generation. The Cherokee Nation offers courses online for those who wish to learn to speak Tsalagi.

Because Indian young people are reluctant to leave their families and travel to distant universities, many nations have established tribal colleges on the reservation. The first to be organized was Navajo Community College, later renamed Diné College, in 1968. Four years later, several tribes came together to form the Indian Higher Education Consortium that successfully lobbied Congress to pass the Tribally Controlled Community College Act in 1978. These community colleges help those Native American students who, because of inadequate preparation in high school, need extra assistance. In 2003, for example, Oglala Lakota College in Kyle, South Dakota, developed a program for American Indian veterans to enable them to "brush up on academics before going on to college."[101] In 2000, the Department of Education created The Native American Vocational and Technical Education Program to offer financial assistance for tuition and books to those Indian students who wish to return to college.[102] Other tribes are talking about creating "virtual colleges," which would take advantage of the online computer lectures provided on some university campuses, sometimes referred to as "distance learning."

Discrimination

The actions mentioned above are necessary because of ongoing racism that sometimes limits scholarship help available to Native American students. McDonald's, the nation's largest fast-food chain, offers minority scholarships, for example, but considers applications only from African Americans, Asian Americans, and Hispanic Americans. For McDonald's, Indians are apparently the forgotten minority.[103] The Supreme Court's

2003 decision that effectively struck down affirmative action as a tool to achieve wider cultural representation on college campuses, has resulted in a 23 percent drop in applications from blacks, Hispanics, and American Indians at the University of Michigan, the original litigant in the case. Admission of minority students is down 30 percent.[104]

Discrimination continues in other areas as well. A 2003 HUD study found that "American Indians are more likely than any other minority group to face discrimination when trying to rent homes . . ."[105] In New Mexico, Montana, and Minnesota, states with large Indian populations, 29 percent of all potential Indian renters were turned away. Such ongoing racism faces Native Americans in American society, another factor in the decision of many to return to the reservation, where their children can grow up sheltered from that sort of brutality. Still, from an early age children are taught where they can go and where they can't, what is safe and what isn't— all part of the reality of being Native American in the United States.

Revitalization

One of the real success stories of recent years lies in the work of Ada Deer and other Menominee leaders, who persuaded Congress to pass the Menominee Restoration Act in 1973. Of the sixty-one tribes terminated in the 1950s, only the Menominee has retrieved its lands and federally recognized reservation status. In March 1976, Wisconsin returned all authority to the Menominee Nation to organize its own court system and oversee hunting and fishing rights on its lands. Now the Menominees may once again operate their lumber mills, using their timber resources to provide jobs for their people. In addition, they have opened a casino, as well as a bingo parlor, but "the lumber mill and the Menominee forests are still the mainstay of reservation employment."[106]

In South Carolina, the Catawba Indian Nation continues to

In the 1970s, Ada E. Deer, who currently serves as the director of the American Indian Studies program at the University of Wisconsin–Madison, was very influential in helping her tribe, the Menominee, regain its lands and federally recognized status after being terminated by the U.S. government in the 1950s. Today, the Menominees run a lucrative lumber industry, as well as a casino.

exist even though the federal tribe status stripped from them by Termination in 1961 has never been restored. Undaunted, the Catawbas remained determined to protect their community. In 2004, they applied for and received a $450,000 grant from the U.S. Fish and Wildlife Service. These funds are being used to purchase approximately two hundred acres of what the Catawbas continue to view as their homeland. There, the

Catawbas will teach the next generation about cultural and conservation practices.[107]

As a result of revenues brought in by gaming and other tribal industries, the building of homes, businesses, and cultural centers has grown significantly on some reservations. The 2004 Construction in Indian Country convention, which was held at the Wild Horse Pass Resort in Arizona, noted that much of this construction reflects a commitment to "building upward with new trends in architectural excellence and reflecting specific tribal cultures." Referring to the Wild Horse Pass Resort, Mary Thomas, Lieutenant Governor of the Gila River Community, urged contractors and tribal leaders to enter negotiations in mutual good faith to preserve Native American heritage. "We put a lot of hard work into designing this resort. We want to utilize this land that we hold so precious to our hearts."[108]

Ongoing Problems

So precious to our hearts—a good phrase to describe how Native Americans view their reservations and homelands. Still, despite recent gains, there is a great deal of work to be done to achieve true economic self-determination. One persistent problem is the fact that many dollars earned on the reservation are spent off of it in nearby communities to which Native Americans must travel to purchase groceries, clothes, cars— just about every consumer good. More attention must be paid to Indian-run businesses to serve the needs of their communities. One of the most obvious omissions is the absence of banks on the reservation. Chester Carl, chief executive of the Navajo Housing Authority, points out that while in non-Indian urban communities banks can be found on every street corner, in Navajo land, an area the size of West Virginia, there are only four bank branches.[109]

Tribal governments are well aware of these problems and are taking steps to attract new industries to their communities.

Meanwhile, the economic benefits of those businesses already in place are being used to provide needed services to reservation citizens. One example is the recent construction of a third helipad in Sallisaw, Oklahoma, to serve the Cherokee Nation's Redbird Smith Community Health Center. Air ambulance service provided by helicopters saves lives.[110] New road construction, tribal scholarships, and improved health-care facilities are among the myriad of improvements pursued by Native American governments using their newfound wealth from business development.

The challenges remain. Far too many Native Americans continue to live well below the federal poverty level. Because of language barriers and, sometimes, cultural taboos, not all take advantage of the improved health care that Native American funds have provided. Type II Diabetes remains an enormous problem, especially among many elderly people who will not come to reservation health centers. Indian women are more likely to die of breast cancer than any other minority group even though incidents of the disease are lower for Native American women than white, black, or Hispanic women. In an outreach effort to persuade Navajo women of the value of preventative health care, the San Juan Medical Foundation recently produced two videos, "Breast Cancer: It Can Be Healed" and "Breast Cancer: The Healing Begins," both narrated in Navajo with English subtitles.[111]

The current era of federal budget cuts to programs designed to aid Native American business development pose another hindrance to their economic endeavors. The states, as well, continue their efforts to erode federal protections and seize large portions of the profits from reservation businesses for themselves. But Indian nations are well aware of the dangers posed by corporate and state greed. Moreover, they are proven survivors, just as determined today—as their ancestors were— to live on as Native Americans, and preserve their identity and the homeland that makes that identity possible. Battles lie ahead but the weapons have changed. Native Americans will use the media, scholarship, tribal coalition groups, and, most of all, the courts to stop further theft of their land and resources, as well as their own economic initiative. "It's not muskets anymore. It's not cannon," explained Matthew Seventh Hawk Thomas, Chief of the Narragansett Tribal Nation in 2003. "It's pens and pencils."[112]

1824   Bureau of Indian Affairs organized under the direction of the U.S. Secretary of War.

1831   *Cherokee Nation v. Georgia*—the U.S. Supreme Court upholds Indian sovereignty.

1849   Indian Affairs transferred from War Department to Department of the Interior.

1869   Initiation of President Ulysses S. Grant's Peace Policy.

1887   General Allotment Act.

1911   Organization of the Society of American Indians founded.

1924   Indian Citizenship Act; *Oklahoma's Poor Rich Indians*— report of the Indian Rights Association.

1928   Meriam Report released.

1929   Construction begins on Skyline Drive and Blue Ridge Parkway in Virginia.

1934   Passage of the Indian Reorganization Act.

1935   Indian Arts and Crafts Board Act.

1938   Passage of Omnibus Tribal Leasing Act.

1944   Organization of the National Congress of American Indians; Pick-Sloan Plan to flood 202,000 acres of Sioux land in Missouri River Basin begins.

1946   Indian Claims Commission established by Congress.

1949   *Unto These Hills* opens, outdoor drama of Cherokee history in North Carolina.

1953   Congress passes Termination Resolution and Public Law 280.

1956   Federal Aid Highway Act.

1960   National Indian Youth Council organized.

1964   Army Corps of Engineers builds Kinzua Dam in New York and Pennsylvania, flooding one-third of the Seneca Allegany Reservation.

1965   Economic Development Administration established under the Public Works and Development Act to promote business development in "distressed areas" (42 U.S.C. 3121); Office of Economic Opportunity established as part of the Great Society program.

1968 American Indian Movement organizes.

1969 Takeover of Alcatraz Island in California.

1970 Mount Rushmore protest in South Dakota; United Indian Development Association of Los Angeles program founded.

1972 The Trail of Broken Treaties; Indian Education Act.

1973 Wounded Knee II.

1974 Indian Financing Act.

1975 Indian Self-Determination and Educational Assistance Act; Council of Energy Resource Tribes (CERT) founded.

1976 Indian Health Care Improvement Act.

1978 Indian Child Welfare Act; Indian Religious Freedom Act; and Indian Civil Rights Act.

1979 Florida Seminoles open Bingo Hall with $10,000 jackpots.

1982 Indian Mineral Development Act; Indian Tribal Government Tax Status Act.

1983 *Florida v. Butterworth*—U.S. 5th Circuit Court of Appeals rules that Florida may not regulate bingo on the Seminole Reservation.

1987 *California v. Cabazon Band of Mission Indians*—U.S. Supreme Court rules that if states permit gambling within their boundaries, they cannot prohibit it on reservations.

1988 Indian Gaming Regulatory Act creates the National Indian Gaming Commission to oversee reservation gambling enterprises and compel Indian nations to enter compacts with state governments.

1998 Indian gaming revenues total $500 million.

2002 290 Indian casinos report a combined profit of $12.7 billion.

Notes

Chapter 1:
Historical Developments among Native Americans

1   Arrell Morgan Gibson, *The American Indian: Prehistory to the Present* (Lexington, Mass.: D.C. Heath and Company, 1980), 339.

2   David Rich Lewis, *Neither Wolf Nor Dog: American Indians, Environment, and Agrarian Change* (New York: Oxford University Press, 1994), 75.

3   For these missionaries, trapping and killing animals out of sight seemed less brutal. Even today, most Americans prefer to buy their hamburgers, sausages, and other meats in pristinely cellophane-wrapped packages, giving little or no thought to what goes on when those animals are butchered.

4   For a good study of a follower of the Native American Church, see Nancy Oestreich Lurie, *Mountain Wolf Woman, Sister of Crashing Thunder: The Autobiography of a Winnebago Indian* (Ann Arbor, Mich.: University of Michigan Press), 1961.

5   Senate Report No. 5013, 59th Congress, 2nd Session, Part I, 180–190, in Steven Mintz, ed., *Native American Voices: A History and Anthology* (St. James, N.Y.: Brandywine Press, 1995), 167.

6   Peter Nabokov, *Native American Testimony* (New York: Penguin/Putnam, Inc., 1991), 306.

Chapter 2:
Self-Determination

7   United States Census, April 1, 2004; accessible at *factfinder.census.gov*. For more information, see the U.S. Census Bureau's website at *www.census.gov/population/www/socdemo/race/indian/html*

8   U.S. Bureau of the Census (Washington, D.C., August 1995).

9   "TM-POO 4C, Percentage of Persons Who are American Indian and Alaska Native Alone: 2000," U.S. Bureau of the Census (Washington, D.C., April 1, 2004).

10 *United States v. Rogers*, 1846.

11 *Eastern Band of Cherokee Indians v. U.S. and Cherokee Nation, West*, 1886.

12 Mark N. Trahant, "The Center of Everything," *Seattle Times*, June 4, 1999.

13 William N. Thompson, *Native American Issues: A Reference Handbook* (Santa Barbara, Calif.: ABC-CLIO, Inc., 1996), 21.

14 "Tribes Accuse County of Excluding American Indians From Jobs," The Associated Press, March 19, 2004.

15 Arrell Morgan Gibson, *The American Indian: Prehistory to the Present* (Lexington, Mass.: D.C. Heath and Company, 1980), 558.

16 Peter Nabokov, *Native American Testimony* (New York: Penguin Putnam, Inc., 1999), 356.

17 After the governor ordered the game wardens to destroy all Indian camps along the river, Gregory and others were released early.

18 Colin Calloway, *First Peoples: A Documentary Survey of American Indian History* (Boston, Mass.: Bedford/St. Martin's, 2004), 469.

19 For a good study of LaDonna Harris, see Gary C. Anderson, "LaDonna Harris," *The New Warriors: Native American Leaders since 1900*, ed. R. David Edmunds (Lincoln, Nebr.: University of Nebraska Press, 2001), 123–144.

20 Ibid, 134.

21 Peter Iverson, *The Navajo Nation* (Albuquerque, N.M.: University of New Mexico Press, 1981), 130–131.

Chapter 3:
Tourism

22 For more information about the Museum of the Cherokee Indian, please visit *www.cherokeemuseum.org*. To learn about other tourism opportunities in and around the Qualla Boundary, visit *www.cherokee-nc.com*.

23 Penobscot spokesman Newell Francis in an interview with the *Lewiston (ME) Evening Journal* (July 30, 1921), found in Bunny McBride, "Lucy Nicolar: The Artful Activism of a Penobscot Reformer," *Sifters: Native American Women's Lives*, ed. Theda Perdue (New York: Oxford University Press, 2001), 149.

24 49 U.S. Statute 891, August 27, 1935. 104 U.S. Statute 4662 gave the board increased authority in 1990.

25 Peter Iverson, *The Navajos* (New York: Chelsea House Publishers, 1990), 53–54.

26 Jake Sandlin, "NLR Sees New Tie to Trail of Tears; City to Incorporate Link in Birthday Bash, Maritime Museum," *Arkansas Democrat-Gazette*, April 27, 2004.

27 For one example, see Henry Farber, "Native American Heritage Day: Treasured Legacy; Celebration Showcases Skills, Culture of Forebears," *Atlanta Journal-Constitution,* April 15, 2004.

28 Marjane Ambler, "The Importance of Economic Development on the Reservation," *Major Problems in American Indian History,* eds. Albert L. Hurtado and Peter Iverson (Lexington, Mass.: D.C. Heath and Company, 1994), 551.

29 For examples of this work, see Colin Calloway, "Twentieth-Century Indian Artists Depict Indian Life," *First Peoples: A Documentary Survey of American Indian History* (Boston, Mass.: Bedford/St. Martin's, 2004), 456–463.

30 One example is *www.alaskanativeartists.com,* sponsored by the Sealaska Heritage Institute, a non-profit group that hosts the site to enable buyers to purchase directly from thirteen Native American artists.

31 On one occasion I stopped for a young woman who had already been walking for hours. I had spotted her car several miles back. White skin turns red quickly in the Southwest desert (leading to the inevitable Indian jokes about who is the real Redskin). By the time I found her, this girl already bore a close resemblance to a lobster. Turns out she was getting married the next day and, suffering the common cold feet that everyone experiences before the "big event," had come out to drive around the reservation to think. The wedding went off the next day without a hitch, although the bride had to walk down the aisle with a heck of a sunburn.

32 Kanuchi is made with pulverized hickory nuts. It takes a lot of work and most folks use the flour to make balls, about three inches in size, and freeze them for future use. To make kanuchi, one boils one of the balls in about a quart of water before straining the mixture and adding hominy. Some people use rice, but in the South, grits are the usual ingredient of choice. Most add corn syrup or molasses to sweeten and serve the dish as a hot soup.

33 Alan L. Sorkin, *American Indians and Federal Aid* (Washington, D.C.: The Brookings Institute, 1971), 1.

Chapter 4:
Energy Development

34 Calloway, *First Peoples: A Documentary Survey of American Indian History* (Boston, Mass.: Bedford/St. Martin's, 2004), 477–478.

35 Gibson, *The American Indian,* 508.

36 Iverson, *The Navajos,* 86.

37 Donald L. Fixico, "Tribal Leaders and the Demand for Natural Energy Resources on Reservation Lands," *The Plains Indians of the Twentieth Century* (Norman, Okla.: University of Oklahoma Press, 1985), 222.

38 Calloway, *First Peoples,* 479.

39 Vine Deloria, Jr. and Clifford Lytle, *The Nations Within: The Past and Future of American Indian Sovereignty* (New York: Pantheon Books, 1984), 256.

40 Brenda Norrell, "Scientists Back Navajos Fighting Uranium Mining," *Indian Country Today,* March 12, 2004.

41 Robert Gehrke, "Appeals Court Lets Tribe Continue Pursuit of $600 Million in Coal Royalties," The Associated Press State and Local Wire, October 25, 2003. See also, Fixico, "Tribal Leaders and the Demand for Natural Energy Resources on Reservation Lands," 230.

42 Lauren Donovan, "Sioux Get Hearing on Mine," *Bismarck Tribune,* May 27, 2004.

43 Brenda Norrell, "National Congress of American Indians Debates Energy Bill," *Indian Country Today,* December 3, 2003.

44 Susan Montoya Bryan, "National Congress of American Indians Ask Senate to Kill Energy Bill," The Associate Press State and Local Wire, November 20, 2003.

45 Calloway, *America's First Peoples,* 481.

46 Beth Daley, "Maine Tribe Invites LNG Facility; Some See Terminal As Economic Boon," *Boston Globe,* July 5, 2004.

47 Calloway, *First Peoples,* 483.

48 For a good study of both sides of the Campo issue, see Dan McGovern, *The Campo Indian Landfill War: The Fight for Gold in California's Garbage* (Norman, Okla.: University of Oklahoma Press, 1995).

49 Pamela Wood, "Landfill Sale to Indian Tribe May Be Tricky," *Maryland Gazette,* April 28, 2004.

Chapter 5:
Business Development

50 For an in-depth look at the Navajo Stock Reduction, see Iverson, *The Navajo Nation.*

51 See Michael Lawson, *Dammed Indians: The Pick-Sloan Plan and the Missouri River Sioux, 1944–1980* (Norman, Okla.: University of Oklahoma Press, 1982). For more information about how the Seneca Nation will never forget what happened at Kinzua, consult *www.sni.org.* See also Joy Bilharz, *The Allegany Senecas and Kinzua Damn: Forced Relocation through Two Generations* (Lincoln, Nebr.: University of Nebraska Press, 1998).

52 David L. Vines, "Cultural Values and Economic Development on Reservations," in *American Indian Policy in the Twentieth Century*, ed. Vine Deloria, Jr. (Norman, Okla.: University of Oklahoma Press, 1985), 156.

53 For a good short study of the Menominees, highly suitable for classroom use, see Patricia K. Ourada, *The Menominee* (New York: Chelsea House Publishers, 1990).

54 Donald L. Fixico, *Urban Indians* (New York: Chelsea House Publishers, 1991), 71.

55 Minutes of the Joint Business Council meeting, April 30, 1969. Records of the BIA, Fort Washakie, Wyoming. Found in Loretta Fowler, "'What They Issue You:' Political Economy at Wind River," in *The Plains Indians of the Twentieth Century*, ed. Peter Iverson (Norman, Okla.: University of Oklahoma Press, 1985), 192.

56 The federal government's Economic Development Agency makes funds available for constructing businesses in "depressed areas" provided those companies have the consent of the community. The poverty rates on most reservations certainly meet those qualifications.

57 For a good study of the Arapaho Reservation and economics there, see Loretta Fowler, *Arapaho Politics: 1851–1978: Symbols in Crisis of Authority* (Lincoln, Nebr.: University of Nebraska Press, 1982). For a succinct overview of the Arapaho suitable for classroom use, see Fowler's *The Arapaho*, part of the Indians of North American Series (New York: Chelsea House Publishers, 1995).

58 "Cherokee Nation to Host Job Fair for Mayes and Rogers Counties," *Cherokee Nation News Release* (April 2, 2004).

59 Deloria and Lytle, *The Nations Within*, 257.

60 Mike Stark, "U.S. Withdraws Support for Indian Ag Program," *Billings (MT) Gazette*, January 15, 2004.

61 "Tribal Representatives Talk about Budget Needs," The Associated Press State and Local Wire, February 12, 2004.

62 Donald L. Fixico, *The Urban Indian Experience in America* (Albuquerque, N.M.: University of New Mexico Press, 2000), 137.

Chapter 6:
Gaming

63 *Florida v. Butterworth* (1983).

64 *California v. Cabazon Band of Mission Indians* (1987).

65 William Thompson, *Native American Issues: A Reference Handbook* (Santa Barbara, Calif.: ABC-CLIO, Inc., 1996), 52.

66 Calloway, *First Peoples*, 486.

67 Ibid, 487.

68 For free brochures describing the many tourist sites available at Cherokee, North Carolina, including the casino, access *www.cherokee-nc.com* or *www.cherokeemuseum.org.* Information about Harrah's operations can be found at *www.harrahs.com.*

69 This information was found in *Indian Gaming*, a magazine that for the last ten years has highlighted casino operations, usually offering a cover story on a specific casino in each issue. For more information, one may e-mail them at *info@igmagazine.com.*

70 "Oneida Nation Pays Out $3.7 Million in Workers' Bonuses," The Associate Press State and Local Wire, December 16, 2003.

71 "Cherokee Casino Will Bring Oklahoma Army National Guardsmen Home for the Holidays," Cherokee Nation enterprises Media advisory, December 22, 2003. For more Cherokee news, please visit *www.cherokee.org.*

72 Associated Press, "Indian Tribes Funding School Projects, Endeavors," *Los Angeles Times*, April 11, 2004.

73 "San Manuel Indians Donate $1 million to Fire Relief Efforts," The Associated Press State and Local Wire, November 3, 2003.

74 "Arizona Tribe Helping Casino Development

in California," The Associated Press State and Local Wire, October 15, 2003.

75 "Indian Tribes Forge Ties with $42 Million Loan," The Associated Press State and Local Wire, November 16, 2003.

76 Mark Shaffer, "Moccasin, Ariz.-Area Tribe Struggles to Survive after Casino Failure," *Indian Country Today*, January 7, 2004.

77 Brenda Norrell, "Hopi Voters Reject Gaming: Votes Lean toward Traditional Path," *Indian Country Today*, May 28, 2004.

78 Michael Mello, "Narragansett Indians Release Plans for $450 Million Casino," The Associated Press State and Local Wire, February 5, 2004.

79 "Tribe Starts New Hotel in Gambling Town," The Associated Press State and Local Wire, December 2, 2003.

80 Patrick Sweeney, "Gambling Comment Tough to Interpret," *Saint Paul (MN) Pioneer Press*, February 6, 2004.

81 Matt Pommer, "AG Calls Bets on Casino Suit," *Madison (WI) Capital Times*, December 8, 2003.

82 Raymond Hernandez, "Trump Named in Inquiry on Financing Indian Groups, *New York Times*, May 6, 2004.

83 Chris Frink, "Foster Leaves Casino Pact on Table," *Baton Rouge (LA) Advocate*, January 7, 2004.

84 Alex Fryer, "Snohomish Stand in Hope of Recognition," *Seattle Times*, November 26, 2003.

Chapter 7:
Sovereignty versus the State

85 "Indian Veterans Sue for Back Pay," The Associated Press State and Local Wire Service, December 10, 2003.

86 Spreck Rosekrans, analyst with Environmental Defense in a letter to the Alameda City Council and Island Residents, quoted in Kristen Bender, "Tribe Asks Alameda to Restore River," *Alameda (CA) Times-Star*, January 17, 2004.

87 James M. Odato, "Senecas' Ads Get Message Across: Tribe Has Spent $2M and Counting on Anti-tax Campaign," *Albany (NY) Times Union*, January 23, 2004.

88 Scott Rapp, "Cayugas Gather Anti-Tax Signatures," *Syracuse (NY) The Post-Standard*, December 4, 2003.

89 Tom Wanamaker, "Seneca Nation Sues New York over Internet Smoke Sales Ban," *Indian Country Today*, January 24, 2004. Readers wishing to learn more about the Seneca Nation are encouraged to visit their website at *www.sni.com*.

90 Mary Reinholz, "Indians and State Near Cigarette Pact," *New York Times*, April 11, 2004.

91 Elizabeth Zuckerman, "Federal Judge Rules State Was Right to Shut Down Smoke Shop," The Associated Press State and Local Wire, December 29, 2003.

92 Public Law 280 (67 U.S. Statue 588) applies to California, Nebraska, Minnesota (except Red Lake Reservation), Oregon (except Warm Springs Reservation), and Wisconsin (except the Menominee Reservation).

93 Louis Sahagun, "Tribes Fear Backlash to Prosperity," *Los Angeles Times*, May 3, 2004.

94 James P. Sweeney, "Deciding Tribes 'Fair Share' May Be Tougher than Expected," Copley News Service, November 7, 2003.

95 Josh Richman, "Tribal Gaming Liaison Named," *Alameda (CA) Times-Star* January 8, 2004.

96 Ben Schnayerson, "Leaders Speak of Political 'Warfare,'" *San Bernardino (CA) Sun News*, January 15, 2004.

97 "Agents Raid Coyote Valley Casino, Tribal Leader Homes Near Ukiah," The Associated Press State and Local Wire, May 27, 2004.

98 Jerry Reynolds, "Analysis: GOP Comes Together on Taxation of Tribes," *Indian Country Today*, March 12, 2004.

99 Anishinaabe leader Marge Anderson responding to Washington Senator Slade Gorton's 1997 bill to require tribes to waive sovereignty, found in Colin Calloway, *First Peoples: A Documentary Survey of American Indian History* (Boston, Mass.: Bedford/St. Martin's, 2004), 470.

Chapter 8:
Owenvsv

100 Fixico, *The Urban Indian Experience in America*, 153.

101 "Program Gives American Indian Vets Chance

Notes

to Polish Academic Skills," The Associated Press State and Local Wire, November 2, 2003.

102 Denyse Clark, "Training Program Offered to American Indians/Three-Year-Old Program has 84 Students Enrolled This Semester," *Rock Hill (SC) Herald*, November 14, 2003.

103 James May, "McDonald's Minority Scholarship Program Omits American Indians," *Indian Country Today*, January 7, 2004.

104 Sarah Freedom, "Minority Applications and Enrollments Drop at Michigan After Affirmative Action Is Ended," The Associated Press State and Local Wire, February 9, 2004.

105 George C. Armas, "Study Finds American Indians Discriminated Against in Rental Market More than Other Groups," The Associated Press, November 18, 2003.

106 Ourada, *The Menominee*, 102.

107 Denyse Clark, "Catawba Indians to Turn

Federal Grant Money Into Land to Hunt, Fish and Educate Their Children," *Rock Hill (SC) Herald*, February 23, 2004.

108 Brenda Norrell, "American Indians' Convention in Arizona Focuses on Booming Construction Sector," *Indian Country Today*, May 19, 2004.

109 Mark Fogarty, "'Unbanked' Population Poses Big Problem in Indian Country," *Indian Country Today*, December 10, 2003.

110 "Cherokee Nation Sallisaw Clinic Received New Helipad," Cherokee Nation News Release, January 29, 2004.

111 Laura Banish, "Breast Cancer More Deadly for Native Americans," The Associated Press State and Local Wire, October 17, 2003.

112 Alfonso A. Castillo, "Tribes Unite in Hamptons; Hundreds Mark Indigenous Day," *Newsday*, November 13, 2003.

Bibliography

Ambler, Marjane. "The Importance of Economic Development on the Reservation." In *Major Problems in American Indian History*, edited by Albert L. Hurtado and Peter Iverson, 545–556. Lexington, Mass.: D.C. Heath and Company, 1994.

Anderson, Gary. "LaDonna Harris, Comanche." In *The New Warriors: Native American Leaders since 1900*, edited by R. David Edmunds, 123–144. Lincoln, Nebr.: University of Nebraska Press, 2001.

Bilharz, Joy A. *The Allegany Senecas and Kinzua Dam: Forced Relocation through Two Generations*. Lincoln, Nebr.: University of Nebraska Press, 1998.

Calloway, Colin. *First Peoples: A Documentary Survey of American Indian History*. Boston, Mass.: Bedford/St. Martin's, 2004.

Deloria, Vine, Jr., and Clifford Lytle. *The Nations Within: The Past and Future of American Indian Sovereignty*. New York: Pantheon Books, 1984.

Edmunds, David R., ed. *The New Warriors: Native American Leaders since 1900*. Lincoln, Nebr.: University of Nebraska Press, 2001.

Fixico, Donald L. "Tribal Leaders and the Demand for Natural Energy Resources on Reservation Lands." In *The Plains Indians of the Twentieth Century*, edited by Peter Iverson, 219–235. Norman, Okla.: University of Oklahoma Press, 1985.

_____. *The Urban Indian Experience in America*. Albuquerque, N.M.: University of New Mexico Press, 2000.

_____. *Urban Indians*. New York: Chelsea House Publishers, 1991.

Fowler, Loretta. *Arapahoe Politics, 1851–1978: Symbols in Crisis of Authority*. Lincoln, Nebr.: University of Nebraska Press, 1982.

_____. *The Arapaho*. New York: Chelsea House Publishers, 1995.

Gibson, Arrell Morgan. *The American Indian: Prehistory to the Present*. Lexington, Mass.: D.C. Heath and Company, 1980.

Iverson, Peter. *The Navajo Nation*. Albuquerque, N.M.: University of New Mexico Press, 1981.

_____. *The Navajos*. New York: Chelsea House Publishers, 1990.

_____, ed. *The Plains Indians of the Twentieth Century*. Norman, Okla.: University of Oklahoma Press, 1985.

Lawson, Michael. *Dammed Indians: The Pick-Sloan Plan and the Missouri River Sioux, 1944–1980*. Norman, Okla.: University of Oklahoma Press, 1982.

Bibliography

Lewis, David Rich. *Neither Wolf Nor Dog: American Indians, Environment, and Agrarian Change.* New York: Oxford University Press, 1994.

Lurie, Nancy Oestreich. *Mountain Wolf Woman, Sister of Crashing Thunder: The Autobiography of a Winnebago Indian.* Ann Arbor, Mich.: University of Michigan Press, 1961.

McBride, Bunny. "Lucy Nicolar: The Artful Activism of a Penobscot Reformer." In *Sifters: Native American Women's Lives,* edited by Theda Perdue, 141–159. New York: Oxford University Press, 2001.

McGovern, Dan. *The Campo Indian Landfill War: The Fight for Gold in California's Garbage.* Norman, Okla.: University of Oklahoma Press, 1995.

Mintz, Steven, ed. *Native American Voices: A History and Anthology.* St. James, N.Y.: Brandywine Press, 1995.

Nabokov, Peter. *Native American Testimony.* New York: Penguin Putnam, Inc. 1999.

Oklahoma's Poor Rich Indians. Philadelphia, Pa.: The Indian Rights Association, 1924.

Ourada, Patricia K. *The Menominee.* New York: Chelsea House Publishers, 1990.

Thompson, William N. *Native American Issues: A Reference Handbook.* Santa Barbara, Calif.: ABC-CLIO, Inc. 1996.

Vines, David L. "Cultural Values and Economic Development on Reservations." In *American Indian Policy in the Twentieth Century,* edited by Vine Deloria, Jr., 155–176. Norman, Okla.: University of Oklahoma Press, 1985.

Websites

www.asu.edu/lib/archives/links.htm

This website, sponsored by Arizona State University, provides one of the most complete set of links this author has found on the Internet. Teachers interested in all American Indian issues should consult this resource.

www.cherokee.org

The official website of the Cherokee Nation offers a number of teaching tools for classroom use as well as the latest tribal news. A recent welcome addition has been the establishment of an online language course for those wishing to learn to speak Tsalagi (the Cherokee language).

www.cradleboard.org

The Cradleboard Teaching Project was founded by Buffy Sainte-Marie to provide social studies teachers with classroom-ready lesson plans. These are organized for elementary school (grades 3–5), middle school (grades 6–8), and high school (grades 9–12) instruction.

www.dpi.state.wi.us/amind/index.html

The State of Wisconsin now requires that its public school social studies curriculum include instruction on American Indian culture. Teachers in other states wishing to learn more about the curriculum established by the Department of Public Instruction in Wisconsin can find it here.

www.geotrees.com/nightwolf.html

Jay Winter Nightwolf, a Washington, D.C., area American Indian offers a weekly radio program that examines many current economic and social issues in Indian country. His broadcast may be heard on Sunday evenings on Washington, D.C.'s WPFW, 89.3 FM (the broadcast is available online at *http://wpfw.org*). His past guests have included tribal officials, as well as leading advocates from groups like the National Congress of American Indians.

www.hanksville.org/Naresources/

This site provides an extensive virtual library on a host of Native American issues.

www.humboldt.edu/~go1/kellogg/NativeRelationship.html

This site provides access to *American Indian Issues: An Introductory and Curricular Guide for Educators*, which was developed by the American Indian Civics project and funded by the W.K. Kellogg Foundation's Native American Higher Education Initiative. Here one may find succinct summaries of a variety of issues dealing with Native Americans' history and current development. The site includes both unit and lesson plans for classroom use.

www.igmagazine.com

Indian Gaming is the national magazine of the American Indian gaming industry. One may subscribe or read excerpts of each issue at this website.

www.indiancountry.com

This site provides an online version of the country's largest American Indian newspaper, *Indian Country Today*, published weekly. One may also subscribe (see site for more information).

www.indiangaming.org

This is the website of the National Indian Gaming Association and provides full news coverage of all activity surrounding gaming issues nationwide.

http://jaie.asu.edu/

The *Journal of American Indian Education* is available through subscription. Its online site offers a synopsis of all volumes back to 1961.

www.ksg.harvard.edu/hpaied/

This website provides information about the Harvard Project on American Indian Economic Development, housed in the John F. Kennedy School of Government.

www.nativeweb.com

Current news about issues affecting Native peoples worldwide may be found on this site, which also provides a multitude of links for information on economic and other issues.

www.newberry.org/mcnickle/darcyhome.html

The D'Arcy McNickle Center for American Indian History at the Newberry Library in Chicago remains one of the best archives in the nation.

www.osu-okmulgee.edu/faculty_and_staff/carsten_schmidtke/indian.htm

An older site that is very user-friendly for teachers and students alike has been created by Carsten Schmidtke at Oklahoma State University–Okmulgee and offers a multitude of links.

www.sni.org

To learn more about the continuing controversy between New York and its Seneca peoples, one may read the latest news at this website of the Seneca Nation.

www.usgs.gov/features/native_americans.html

The United States Geographical Service offers a valuable series of photographs from the Blue Cloud Abbey Native American Photograph collection. Most of these photographs depict early-twentieth-century life in and around the Yankton Sioux Reservation in southeastern South Dakota.

Perhaps the most valuable web resource for teachers interested in learning more about Native Americans today can be found through H-NET, a service of Michigan State University. To register, contact H-AMINDIAN@H-NET.MSU.EDU. Operated by a very capable staff at Arizona State University, H-AMINDIAN will send the latest news releases from wire services, relevant publications, and comments by individuals, for the most part teachers in American Indian studies.

Index

Index

Picture Credits

Deborah Welch, Ph.D., is the Director of the Public History Program and Associate Professor of History at Longwood University. Welch has published numerous books and articles, including *Virginia: An Illustrated History* (Hippocrene Books); "Zitkala-Sa," which appeared in *American National Biography* (Oxford University Press), and "Gertrude Simmons Bonnin," which appeared in *The New Warriors: American Leaders since 1900*. Her fictional mysteries set among American Indian peoples appear under the pseudonym P.D. Lawrence.

Paul C. Rosier received his Ph.D. in American History from the University of Rochester, with a specialty in Native American History. His first book, *Rebirth of the Blackfeet Nation, 1912–1954*, was published by the University of Nebraska Press in 2001. In November 2003, Greenwood Press published *Native American Issues* as part of its Contemporary American Ethnic Issues series. Dr. Rosier has also published articles on Native American topics in the *American Indian Culture and Research Journal*, and the *Journal of American Ethnic History*. In addition, he was a coeditor of *The American Years: A Chronology of United States History*. He is Professor of History at Villanova University, where he also serves as a faculty advisor to the Villanova Native American Student Association.

Walter Echo-Hawk is a member of the Pawnee tribe. He is a staff attorney of the Native American Rights Fund (*www.narf.org*) and a Justice on the Supreme Court of the Pawnee Nation (*www.pawnee nation.org/court.htm*). He has handled cases and legislation affecting Native American rights in areas such as religious freedom, education, water rights, fishing rights, grave protection, and tribal repatriation of Native dead.